UNDONE BY EASTER

UNDONE BY EASTER

KEEPING PREACHING FRESH

WILLIAM H. WILLIMON

Abingdon Press
Nashville

UNDONE BY EASTER
KEEPING PREACHING FRESH

Library of Congress Cataloging-in-Publication Data

Willimon, William H.
    Undone by Easter : keeping preaching fresh / William H. Willimon.
        p. cm.
    Includes bibliographical (p.   ) references and indexes.
    ISBN 978-1-426-70013-2 (binding: pbk./trade pbk., adhesive perfect : alk. paper)
    1. Preaching. I. Title.
    BV4211.3.W535 2009
    251—dc22
                            2009011711

10 11 12 13 14 15 16 17 18—10 9 8 7 6 5 4 3 2

MANUFACTURED IN THE UNITED STATES OF AMERICA

To H. Keith H. Brodie, M.D.

CONTENTS

The proclaimed word has its origin in the incarnation of Jesus Christ. It neither originates from truth once perceived nor from personal experience. It is not the reproduction of a specific set of feelings. . . . The proclaimed word is the incarnate Christ himself . . . the thing itself. The preached Christ is both the Historical One and the Present One. . . . The proclaimed word is not a medium of expression for something else, something which lies behind it, but rather is the Christ himself walking through his congregation as the word.

Dietrich Bonhoeffer, *Worldly Preaching*, ed. Clyde E. Fant (Nashville and New York: Thomas Nelson, 1975), 125.

INTRODUCTION

This is what happened after two thousand sermons. I have attempted to bring the gospel to speech that many Sundays and still plan to say it again Sunday next. This little book arose out of a gracious invitation from Dean L. Gregory Jones to give the 2005 Jamison Jones Lectures at Duke University. My assigned topic was how to keep preaching fresh. I took the challenge. After all, a major concern of most homiletics courses (even though most of the preaching students have preached no more than a dozen sermons) is how to make preaching less dull, how to preach a fourth Easter when you have already told the parishioners all that you know in the last three. There is an undeniable tendency of religious language to diminish over time into platitude and shibboleth. How do we preachers keep from boring ourselves to death, to say nothing of killing the congregation?

Herein I continue my conversation with Karl Barth.[1] How can we preachers proclaim the gospel time and time again without destroying the gospel? The answer lies not in us but in the gospel. Much of my argument is an extended reflection upon the implications of what Barth says in Volume III, part 2 of section 47 ("Man in His Time") of *Church Dogmatics*.

Søren Kierkegaard (S.K.), whom I've been rereading during the past two years (because S.K. disbelieves in just about everything I'm now doing), has also been helpful, but in an annoying sort of way.

I dedicate this book to Dr. H. Keith H. Brodie, who has constantly encouraged me to continue scholarly endeavor, even as a bishop.

One of my episcopal tasks is the somber receiving of credentials of pastors who call it quits. The grind of having to persevere in the gospel, the necessity of having to repeat ourselves, the prospect of next Sunday's sermon relentlessly looming before us sometimes gets to us. How do we preachers summon the nerve to say the same thing about Jesus over and again?

If this book helps some of my sisters and brothers in that task, if it helps our listeners hear the ancient good news as news, then I'll be glad I've said it, again.

William H. Willimon
The Second Sunday of Easter

CHAPTER ONE

NEW

My subject is how to preach the faith of the church—*again?* We preachers repeat ourselves. To be a faithful preacher is to be willing to preach the truth again and yet again. We've got fifty-two Sundays a year, without interruption. *The Common Lectionary* requires texts to roll around again every three years, like clockwork. I've preached the death and resurrection of Jesus repeatedly—at least 135 times (not counting a botched attempt as a seminarian in 1969). I ought to know something of the challenge of preaching even so stirring a story as Good Friday and Easter *again.* The Second Law of Thermodynamics declares that even the most heated outburst of energy immediately entropies. Everything is moving toward average, even the most brilliant sermons.

In one of my early congregations, Hubert Parris could always be counted upon, if the service stirred him, to stand and recount the story of his conversion *again.* He had narrated his conversion so many times I watched as young children mouthed the words before Hubert could repeat them—a little girl on the front row mouthing, in unison with Hubert, "I was sunk in sin. I was lost, lost, I tell you . . . ." The story of Hubert's Damascus Road Experience (which actually occurred on the highway headed toward Gainesville) went limp in the retelling. It was the *again* that got us.

Hubert is us preachers, even on Easter. The modern world makes neophiles of us all. That which is new is self-validated simply by being novel. Truth becomes truth when it is endorsed by my subjective recognition of it as new, by my excited acclamation, "How fabulously *fresh!*" Inner, subjective validation, in which my subjectivity becomes the supreme arbiter of all truth, is just one inheritance of modernity, that epoch that thought it had ended inheritance. Schleiermacher created modern theology when he made "God-consciousness" the proper subject matter for theology. Note that "God" is no longer the concern of

1

theology now but rather our subjective "God-consciousness." Human experience of God is made more interesting than God.

A confession: as a child of modernity, I too am servant of novelty. One of the weaknesses in my preaching is the enjoyment of novelty engendered in me by twenty-five years of ministry in an academic community that tends to confuse innovation with intelligence and to hope that originality is a safeguard against mediocrity. That's the worst sort of book review: "This book tells the truth, but alas, it says nothing new." Every university town is Athens where, to paraphrase Acts 17:21, "they spent their time in talking about something new" (Greek: *kainos*).

I therefore confess a bit too much delight in cleverness—the gospel delivered with a lime twist. I have thrilled to some academic emerging from Sunday at Duke Chapel muttering, "That's *so-o-o interesting!* Haven't heard the story of the prodigal son from the point of view of the fatted calf. How deliciously novel!"

As a young pastor I imbibed Fred Craddock's Beecher Lectures, *Overhearing the Gospel.*[1] Our problem, said Craddock, is that the gospel has been "over heard," preached and preached again until it went limp. We preachers must therefore find that Kierkegaardian ironic side door into the gospel, that stunningly new means of presentation whereby our hearers hear again as if for the first time.

Kierkegaard had the problem of boredom and faith ever before him. S.K. said that he took as his task "reintroducing Christianity into Christendom" after Christian language had become boringly wilted with thoughtless overuse. He attempted this by avoiding traditional Christian language, attempting to speak of the faith "in other words." Having no intention of theological innovation, S.K. wanted to say the same thing that Christianity had always said, but "in other words."[2] The language of the church is bankrupt. Boredom is the great modern malady. Now all must be said "in other words."

Craddock's lectures traded heavily on Kierkegaard's statement that "in a Christian land there is no shortage of information about the gospel, what is needed is a new hearing of the gospel." (I discovered, in my own preaching since the seventies, that this is *not* a "Christian land" and there *is* a "shortage of information about the gospel.") Notice that what's needed is, according to S.K.'s construal of preaching, something about us rather than something about the gospel.

Back in the seventies, pastors were either guardians of the tradition—the faith delivered by the saints—or young bucks (like me and my buddies) who assaulted the tradition and mocked the saints.[3] Today I spend most Sundays in congregations who are contemptuous of tradition, empty their auditoria of all historic Christian symbols, and try to look as much like a mall as possible, or as some say on their signs out front, "church for people who hate church."

"Take off that tie!" shouts an usher as I make my way in from the parking lot. "Do you take your latte with a touch of amaretto?" It is so much easier to change that which we fear (the gospel) than to risk change in ourselves by someone as challenging as Jesus.

All but one of my most rapidly growing congregations see themselves as aggressively innovative, making all things new. Churches that once prided themselves on being careful custodians of the past and cautious protectors of the status quo, have now become celebrators of and aggressive advocates for the current age. The eager discovery of "the next thing," once the province of theological liberals, has now become the specialty of so-called Evangelicals. Theological minimalism and reductionism among Evangelicals, where everything about the faith is reduced to "the message," conspire to produce a naive, enthusiastic embrace of the media of contemporary culture in worship with little worry that the content of Christian worship may be radically changed in the experiment.

Neophilia has become the status quo demanded by a capitalist economy. Neither Scripture nor the Christian tradition told these churches that "new" is the chief virtue of a church. What passes these days for new tends to be an uncritical capitulation to the culture, subservience to a "tradition" of the past three decades under the guise of innovation. In loving the new more than Jesus, we lay bare our deep accommodation to a capitalist culture. The market demands new in order to keep functioning. More consumers than believers, we shop for the "new and improved model" of faith "that works for me." Any church that acts like a shopping mall is sure to be treated that way.

Don't you find it curious that High Holy Days get "old" mostly for us preachers? Most of our people come to church on Christmas or Easter hoping to sing the same old hymns, to hear a familiar story.[4] No layperson ever asked, "Easter? *Again?*" Most laity come to church on these high days hoping it *will* all be "again."

Is our boredom with the gospel simply an occupational hazard of being a preacher, of having to handle holy things repeatedly until they droop? Are our laity on to something in their inchoate sense that here our faith rises or falls, that here we are at the center of the story that can't be improved or expanded but only be reiterated? Perhaps our laity, failing to receive the benefits of a first-rate theological education, are less well defended against Jesus than we clergy, therefore to them, the good news of Jesus Christ stays news.

The Temptation of New

In 1913 the French writer Charles Péguy exuberantly pronounced "the world has changed less since the time of Jesus Christ than it has in the last thirty years."[5] The birth of modernity was accompanied by unparalleled hubris.[6] At last humanity had succeeded in doing something wonderfully new, newer than Jesus.

Modernity's self-congratulatory spirit was contested just a few years later by a bloody, pointless war, the invention of modernity's new world order. The brave new world—seen from the muddy mess of World War I—was cruel on a scale unknown in warfare thanks to a deadly concoction of the technological discoveries with the political science of modernity. And soon afterward the Second World War demonstrated that, morally speaking, we had learned little from the First. The modern world gave us not only better and bigger bombs but also the philosophical means to deploy them against civilians without even a twinge of conscience. Of course, like all modern wars, both World Wars were fought in order to make the world a better place.

Prominent German theologians told us that Christianity had overcome the primitive, archaic faith of Israel. Jews were not only questionable citizens of the New Germany but also relegated to the worst of fates—their religion was vestigial, out-of-date. Nazi ideologues exhibited the more somber side of the grand European Enlightenment.[7] Voltaire not only gave us a world in which God had been left behind as the world moved onward and upward but also the bloodiest century we had ever known. Voltaire's snide references to the Jews were somehow connected to the smoke of Dachau. As Dostoevsky ironically commented, without God, anything is possible.

The self-importance of the modern, the sense that humanity was making all things new, continues into the present day which some call "postmodern." Postmodernity may be the latest phase of modernity's faith that novelty is progress, that destruction of the old is necessary to make way for the new and improved model, and that we are—all evidence to the contrary—progressing forward. What is called "postmodern" may simply be modernity raised to an even higher level of hubris—"most-modern."[8]

Art critic Robert Hughes says that the primary emblem of the modern was the Eiffel Tower, finished in 1889, built as the centerpiece for the Paris World's Fair—a grand mechanical exhibition on the centenary of the godless French Revolution. Gustave Eiffel (an engineer, not an architect) designed a great tower with its top in the heavens (Genesis 11:1-9 leaps to mind) that would thrust itself, phallic-like, into the now emptied heavens. Having tamed the earth as our dominion, *la France moderne* would now claim the air. The past—previously esteemed by the human race—became the enemy, something limited and earthbound, something dreadful to be defeated. The tower would support a radio antenna, the source of new, humanly engendered revelation in a world now bereft of a Revealer. The poet Guillaume Apollinaire, ex-Catholic, in a mocking poem compared the tower to the Second Coming of Christ. Where Christ once left the earth to ascend into the heavens, now the tower "climbs skywards like Jesus," leading all blessed modern humanity in its wake.[9]

A century after Péguy it is more difficult for us to muster ebullient delight in the *avant-garde*. The ascent of the tower was followed by a plummet into the grubby trenches of the Great War. About the time that work was begun on the glorious new tower, we invented the recoil-operated machine gun.

Not everyone thought positively about the new and the modern. Back in 1818 Mary Shelley wrote *Frankenstein*. Some warned that the mechanical paradise would lead to a desolate hell. Today when we see an automobile, we tend not to think of one giant step forward for humanity but rather of toxic pollution, a mechanical servant that has become our menacing master. It's difficult to get anyone to say a good word for the godless, technologically induced future other than intellectual throwbacks like Richard Dawkins or Christopher Hitchens.[10] For those who think more deeply, modernity appears anything but grand.[11] The new has been subjected to almost a century of critique as we learned the hard truth that not every step forward is evolutionary progress and that in each new dawning day, while something is gained, something is lost and the loss may be painful.[12] The modern notion (a mix of Enlightenment and Romantic delusions) that history is actually moving somewhere—onward and upward—has been exchanged for postmodern cynicism that history is going nowhere.

The real killer of the idea of progress is evil. As a young pastor, Karl Barth picked up the morning newspaper and there read a "Declaration of Support" for the Imperial German war effort, a statement signed by some of his most admired seminary professors. That declaration made Barth question what he had been taught by his professors, realizing that all of his received theology was tainted by the lies of modernity. Thus began Barth's great theological rebirth, which was also an escape from the debilitating grip of the new.

As Liberal Protestantism dies, the last words upon its lips are, "Progressive Christianity."[13] In modernity, even those who are falling down and backward have the illusion that they are climbing upward and forward.[14] "Progressive Christianity" will never take hold in Germany. *Progressive* is a peculiarly American appellation for the Christian faith, sign of our failure to come to terms with the somber side of modernity. The Germans learned too much about themselves—the hard way—in the twentieth century, to think of the term *progressive* as anything but ugly.

The Christian story is not about humanity gradually, but surely, going onward and upward—Progressive Christianity!—but rather about a God who descends in the darkness to rescue humanity from its downward spiraling plight.

The Temptation to Be at Home in Time

The Bible is obsessed with time, containing over eight hundred references to the subject. While Scripture frequently depicts sacred places, holy space, it more often is concerned with sacred time. "What, then, is time?" asked Augustine. He answered that he knew well enough what time is, but if anybody asked him to explain time "I am baffled."[15] Although I respect the difficulty of attempting to analyze time, much less explain it, even for so great a mind as Augustine, I doubt that many of us really know, even inchoately, what time is, or more importantly, what time is now. One of the pressing questions before the church, anytime we gather, is "What time is it?"

The world's time is not kept by the church. "The church is not the world." On this "humble fact," says James McClendon, theology begins.[16]

John Howard Yoder said that the church has friction with the world because what Scripture names as "world" is "structured unbelief," a "demonic blend of order and revolt"[17] from the world's true Lord. The world's time is a component in Yoder's "demonic blend." As Karl Barth said (in *Evangelical Theology*), "Israel means 'contend against God,' not 'contend for God.'" The church's contention against God takes many forms. One form of Constantinian resistance to the gospel is to sanctify the world's order, to become dependable patriots rather than restless pilgrims, for the church to be at home in the world's time. Yoder called it the "Solomonic Temptation"—the sacralization of the emperor's time in order to make the state the functional equivalent of God. Visit the mall in Washington, D.C., and you will note large, heavy, pagan-inspired granite buildings, all bigger than they need to be, all made to look as if the United States is eternal, as if Thomas Jefferson is forever.

There is a reason our civic architecture is indebted to imperial Rome. Classical literature, philosophy, and art have as their theme the capturing of the eternal. Pagan civilization rests upon the fear, expressed as a question by Aristotle: "Can it be that all things pass away?"[18] By thinking this, or building that, or endowing this chair in the university (or publishing this important book!) we shall not die. We shall go on forever. We have it in our hands—through Platonic philosophy or steel frame construction, to be immortal.

The first three miracles in John's Gospel are Jesus' direct challenge to three great gods of the imperial world—Dionysus who presumed to have a monopoly on turning water to wine, Demeter who thought that she was the source of bread, and Asclepius who reputedly managed the health care delivery system. My point here is that Jesus also challenged Chronos, retrieving time from the grip of a fake god. True, Scripture definitely depicts time as the cycle of recurring seasons, natural time (Gen 1:5, 2:1-3; Eccl 1:4; Ps 78:5-7). Yet the Bible seems more concerned with disrupted, eschatological time, time in which God takes time for God's own purposes, thus disrupting cyclic, natural time (Mark 1:15; 2 Corinthians 6:2).

As William Cavanaugh notes, the purpose of the Constantinian (that is, pagan) eternality project was to make ourselves at home in the world's time.[19] Caesar has a stake in people believing that the cyclic passage of natural time is all there is. Cavanaugh calls Constantinianism "an eschatological heresy." This age, as we have developed it, is normal. There is nothing more. What we have built will last. It is normal. We shall be like gods, for what does any pagan want of a god other than eternality?

Charles Taylor demonstrates that secular political society (the political order in which we moderns now live) could not work without enforcement of a strictly secular (that is, Godless) view of time.[20] Contemporary states presume that civil society occurs in "ordinary historical time" as the achievements of ordinary women and men rather than having any sacral, extrahistorical establishment in "higher time" either by heroic founders (as in the case of Remus and Romulus in Rome) or by God and King David (as in the case of Jerusalem). This "radical horizontality," as Taylor calls it, made God into an ahistorical abstraction. God is still a sort of vague, primordial "Creator" who inspires a degree of awe, but any sense of particular providential care or miraculous intervention is absent. The official "god" of the secular state is an indescribable, therefore undemanding, timeless "mystery." Thus, the modern state virtually required God to be outside of the modern state's time and, therefore, irrelevant. The modern state demands that we first believe that this time is all there is in order to convince us that all there is is the state. We have no time but Caesar's, no God but Caesar.

On the other hand, Barth declared that "humanity is temporality."[21] Humanity is that species for whom the past vanishes, the present is an enigma, and the future is unknown. We literally don't have time. Time has us. Behind us is time lost, and before us is time unknown. All of our achievements (including our invention of the modern state) are trivialized by time. Kant noted that everything "is" only for a moment. After that, everything is only "it was." The fleeting present alone is "real"; all else is a play of thought. Schopenhauer said that time made human existence empty because of the daily human experience that "at every moment, all things become as nothing and thereby lose their true value."[22] Barth says that humanity, as time-bound, time-dominated finite creatures, "has no beyond."[23] Time makes the "Thousand Year Reich" a lie. We have arisen from dust and, even now, we are rapidly returning to dust. The great Julius Caesar, strutting about on the stage of history, is now undistinguished dirt. All we have is the moment and, even as I have written this on my computer, this moment is no more. We have no beyond. Humanity is momentary, inextricably temporal.

Only God has a beyond. Only God can do something about our human problem with time. When the Word was made flesh, eternity took time, defeated time's futility. We are surrounded by nothingness that is time lost,

> But when the fullness of time had come, God sent his Son, born of a woman, born under the law, in order to redeem those who were under the law, so that we might receive adoption as children. . . . So you are no longer a slave but a child, and if a child then also an heir, through God. (Gal 4:4-5, 7)

We are not redeemed *away* from time but as Paul says here in Galatians, God moves *into* time, adopts our time, redeems us from bondage to time's ravages, and generates "the fullness of time." That's the main reason the church attempts to help us take time in the name of Jesus by demanding that we follow the church year. The church teaches us to mark time according to Epiphany, Lent, and Easter rather than as Fourth of July, Thanksgiving, and Mother's Day. We are thereby encouraged not to escape time (as in some Eastern religions) but rather to live in time as those who know what time it really is.

Many have noted the peculiar tendency of the Gospel narratives to locate themselves in a particular geography, constantly mentioning place names and specific geographic locations that no one has ever heard of or is likely to hear of again. The Incarnation is thus demonstrated by Judea, Bethlehem, and Galilee as typical of a God who locates. Note how the Gospels also take pains to state that Jesus occurred not only in place but also in time. "The next day . . . ," "It was about the third hour . . . ." "Immediately . . . ." "On the Sabbath . . . ." "It was night . . . ." In Jesus Christ, God takes time, our time.

From Jews, Christians got the notion that time begins and ends in God's own good time. Christians claim that God became flesh, entered time, and died. Then God raised Jesus from the dead and thereby broke time's sovereignty, disarmed Chronos, unmasked time (Col 2:13-15). That victory is known as resurrection—old time's defeat. In the resurrection our comfortable normality was exposed, eternal-looking temples collapsed, gods were put to rout, and eternality was presented, not as a possible human achievement but rather as pure divine gift. In the resurrection, so we believe, God gave us that which we could never have on our own—a beyond.[24]

And yet, what was the first act of the two apostles after they witnessed the aftermath of resurrection? They went back home (John 20:10)! They attempted to get back to normal. Whenever the emperor's official time is disrupted, we immediately move into action and try to "get back to normal." Homeostasis—that is, static time, uneventful, eternal time—tends to be the goal of most every human undertaking, including the church. We so want things to be predictable, tied down, fixed. Death is the end result of our time, the main reason why nothing that is, is forever. And given a little time, with the help of stoic resignation, we can get used even to death.

Against our deadly accommodation, in the resurrection, death was disarmed and time was taken by God. The end, the future, is in Easter commandeered by God. Time disrupted, eventful is Jesus' time; time under the illusion of normalcy and eternality is Caesar's time. In discussions of war, I have noted, a major argument against pacifism is that "war is hell, has always been hell, and this war is too. Big deal." The violence of war is normal, unavoidable, and the way things are, reality. This defense of war shows a failure to think, a disregard of the history of war and the current practices of war. It is nihilism meant to establish Caesar's time as normal and inevitable.

It is of the nature of the Trinity to disrupt time, to rob Caesar's time of its vaunted claims of inevitability.[25] Time in the Gospels seems compressed, heated, fast-paced, and not only in the Gospel of Mark (whose favorite chronological word is "immediately," *euthys*). It takes Mel Gibson's movie two hours to belabor what Mark does in less than five minutes. One of the reasons we read the Gospels in church is to read ourselves into this peculiar, heated, frenetic gospel time.[26] When Jesus Christ voluntarily submitted to death on the cross, rather than confront Caesar with Caesar's weapons, he thereby robbed Caesar of the illusion that Caesar's time is normal.

In exile, with no future, Israel had her end named as her beginning: "Remember ye not the former things. . . . Behold, I will do a new thing" (Isa 43:18-19 KJV). God is taking back time. In Constantinianism the present social order, the state, is seen as more real, more normal, more eternal, than the reign of God. Peace is then defined as what can reasonably be expected of the state, justice as the accomplishment of the lesser of possible evils, progress is that which a reasonably well-functioning administration might possibly deliver. Under Constantinianism the supreme theological virtue is "realism." (I think this accounts for the enthusiastic support of the Iraq war by University of Chicago theologian Jean Bethke Elshtain. War is the major means of achieving security—security defined as the secure continuance of the state.[27]) As John

Howard Yoder said of the world after Constantine, the concept of the millennium was pulled back from the future (whether distant or imminent) into the present. All that God can possibly have in store for a future victory is more of what has already been won by the empire.[28] And we have shown, in Iraq and elsewhere, that we will defend the status quo, for all its limitations, with murderous intensity, calling that "freedom."

What's now is normal. Joel Osteen's best-selling book is *Your Best Life Now!* Now is the time for the "best." Now is as good as it gets. Marcus Borg similarly collapses eschatology in his attack upon "otherworldly" notions of salvation. Borg says that, "Salvation means to be saved from our predicament in this world."[29] Now. Here. People on top, people in power, tend to be threatened by talk about alternative futures, preferring to construe their now as God's.[30]

Sometimes the attempt to normalize the official present—what is— takes another tack in which the new age of Christ is relegated exclusively to the future, so that since the old age is all-powerful over us, we must adjust ourselves to whatever the current administration is good enough to give us now. The great chronological heresy of Constantinianism is not only its assertion of the normalcy of the now but also its assertion of progress, development.

So-called Progressive Christianity is the latest chapter in our attempts to trim gospel time to the world's time, to denude time, to empty time so there is no agency other than ours.[31] They have thoughtlessly adopted the adjective *progressive* and attached it to Christianity without any apparent awareness of the theological ambiguities in the concept of progress from a Christian perspective.[32] Progress, our progress, becomes the functional equivalent of God. We assume, in modern fashion, that the past is an inadequate, lesser experience of reality and that we are progressing onward, upward to reality in a greater degree. We are gaining on our goal of being God. (I find it odd that, just over half a century from Hiroshima and Dachau, there are Christians who use *progressive* in a positive way.)

Or we go for inner piety, reducing God's promised future to personal experience, or a philosophical ideal, or the church invisible. All of this is meant to disembody and permanently postpone Christian hope. I even worry that the current infatuation with "spiritual practices" could be just another attempt to normalize time—since God is absent and silent, follow these practices to keep busy now in order to sanctify the present order as that which God intends for all time. Some of the "spiritual practices" being urged upon us seem effete, too tame for a people who are evoked by the wild, untamable Word. The spiritual practices needed by preachers are those that give us the guts to be in conversation with, and to speak up for, a true and living God who loves to meet people through the Word. Where the word of God is rightly preached, said Luther, demons are unleashed. I therefore resonate with Marva Dawn's characterization of prayer by preachers as "battling the demons."[33] The great P. T. Forsyth emphasized that preachers require a peculiar kind of prayer life. Prayer for the "preacher . . . is only serious searching prayer, not prayer as sweet and seemly devotion at the day's dawn or close, but prayer as an ingredient of the day's work, pastoral and theological prayer, priest's prayer."[34]

Islam, as well as any faith I know, has marvelous spiritual disciplines for taking over time in the name of God. The faithful follower prays to God throughout the day, stops everything and prays. It must be a marvelous way of taking time for God. Similar disciplines are practiced in monastic spirituality as the Psalms are prayed through in the course of a day. Mainstream Christianity has generally taken a different view. We do not, perhaps we cannot, take time for God. God in Christ takes time *for us* and interrupts, takes time *from us*. God does not wait, thank God, for us to fine-tune the spiritual disciplines to the point where we are praying all day long. Rather, God grants us the freedom to be about our vocations in the world, doing what we have to do in this life. Then, while we journey (Acts 9, the call of Saul), God suddenly shows up, unexpectedly becomes an event in our time, takes our time, disrupts our lives for God. While we are busy planning a wedding, God interrupts, impregnates, and enlists a young woman in a revolution (Luke 2). Eventually, God promises really to take all time from us, that is, all of us shall die and be subsumed into God-determined time, like it or not.

This is how we can say that Christian worship is not primarily, not at its core, something that we do. Rather, our worship is something that God does for us, in us, often despite us. Today's talk about "spiritual practices" could be just one more in our long line of attempts to take time on our terms. Thank God that we don't have to cultivate a tedious set of practices in order to live in God's time. God takes time.

Time Made Strange

Classical Greek religion (that is, most of what we call *philosophy*) attempted to connect us with the divine, to think rationally and thereby to escape contingency, to rise above flux and instability and to flee the ravages of time into a Platonic eternity of thought that is impervious to mortality and the passage of time.

Kierkegaard was among the first (I presume) to note that the Jewish and Christian views of time are very different from the pagan. In Christianity the believer seeks not to rise above time or to escape time but rather to hear the command of God in time, like Abraham heard God calling him on a starry night. Is that why the synoptic Gospels begin with relinquishment, with Jesus' demand to let go of jobs, to abandon marriage and family, and to follow him into an unknown, never predefined destination? Time flows along normally until Jesus sets foot on the scene.

The Greeks marveled that time was full of pattern, recurrence and the eternal return. The first historian, Thucydides, said that the task of the historian was to sort through the flux of time and place, the confusing, odd particularities of human events and find universally recurring patterns. Armed with knowledge of these patterns, the historian could rise above the seeming senselessness of contemporary events and, because one had uncovered the eternally recurring patterns of human history, one could predict how future events would go. Nietzsche's "myth of eternal return" was something similar—this world is finite, closed, bearing within it only a limited number of possible combinations. True newness is impossible. What appears to us as "new" is only the cyclical recurrence of every finite situation an infinite number of times, said Nietzsche.[35] There's nothing new under the sun; it's just the same old thing again and again because all that happens in time is left up to us.

Thucydides and Nietzsche also imply that truth comes through theory, by discovering, through reason and abstraction, that which is universally, eternally true. Detached contemplation is therefore the platonic best way to think. Intellectual discovery is not really discovery of something genuinely new, but rather the uncovering of pattern and order that leads to predictability and understanding. In Plato's *Euthyphro*, Socrates catches an earnest young man on his way to rat on his father for killing a slave. Euthyphro is sure that he is doing the pious (that is, the good) thing. Socrates is not so sure. He asks the young man if his action is right and good because the gods love it and, therefore, it is good or do the gods love it because what he is doing is good? And you know that Plato favors the latter. Plato believes that an action is good because it is inherently good. It is in the structure of reality. It is not part of time but serenely above time. It is eternally good, always and everywhere, for everyone. Even the gods must bow to what is real, that is, to what is eternal.

Kierkegaard realized that Plato was more in love with eternality and abstract ideas of good than in love with the gods. Against Plato, Kierkegaard recalled the story of Abraham's near sacrifice of his son Isaac. Did Abraham think that he ought to offer God his only son because such an act is built into the structure of reality and is therefore always and everywhere good? No. Abraham feels commanded by God, at that time and that place, to commit this act. There is no suggestion that what Abraham does or refrains from doing is applicable to everyone everywhere, noted Kierkegaard. Abraham acts upon a command of God in that specific time and place because nothing is real, nothing has eternality but God.

This is the peculiar sort of truth—God—that is found by practicing truth, embodying truth, engaging in life in a certain time and place. From a biblical point of view, argued Kierkegaard, truth is that which is to be obeyed, not simply that which is contemplated with serene detachment. Truth for the Greeks means that which is most general, most universal and free from time, that which is to be contemplated. Truth for the Hebrews is local and historical, a form of summons, not for everybody, a vocation in time, not above time.[36] Truth for Jews and Christians is found not in detached, sublime contemplation of the ideal but rather in obedience to this God amid the tug and pull of this time and this place.

Theologian Robert Jenson shows that Jews and Christians have a very peculiar idea of what it means for God to be "eternal":

> The biblical God's eternity is his temporal infinity. . . . What [God] transcends is any limit imposed on what can be by what he has been, except the limit of his personal self-identity, and any limit imposed on his action by the availability of time. The true God is not eternal because he lacks time, but because he takes time. . . . [God] is not eternal in that he secures himself from time, but in that he is faithful to his commitments within time. At the great turning, Israel's God is eternal in that he is faithful to the death, and then yet again faithful. God's eternity is temporal infinity.[37]

The Greeks presumed that outsiders, barbarians, could be brought to the truth of things—provided they were willing to learn Greek. Socrates demonstrated this by teaching a mere slave boy—Meno—to do geometry. The Hebrews, on the other hand, treated foreigners as idol worshipers who couldn't become people of the Covenant because they had not been invited by Yahweh to do so. God had shown a sort of serene particularity, here, now in choosing the Hebrews for a Covenant but not others. The faith of Israel shows few aspirations to be a universal religion. Nor was Hebrew morality commended as universally applicable for everyone. This is the way that the people of the Covenant behave after having their time commandeered by God.

Contemporary Evangelicals, therefore, make a big mistake to say that Christianity is absolute truth in the face of alleged postmodern relativity. Jewish-Christian truth is relative to whatever God says. Nothing is true until God speaks. God is not to be found outside of time, absolute, but God descends to time and speaks, reveals, commands, demands, and summons. What's good is good because God commands this in this time and place. Such truth is always relative to the God we've got. Such truth wants to be obeyed rather than contemplated. Obeyed now.

Time and Preaching

I have this on my mind because there appears to be a new form of preaching, unknown in the entire history of Christendom, that for lack of a better term I call "PowerPoint Preaching." I'm talking about the computer program that adeptly throws images and words on a screen. PowerPoint has become the new preacher's essential assistant in communicating of the gospel.

You need not buy a projector to do PowerPoint Preaching. What you do is take some biblical text and boil it down to no less than three "biblical principles," or a set of "Purposes for a Better Life," or "Guides for a Better Marriage," or "Six Steps to More Fulfilling Sex." Sometime ago I edited a collection of sermons from Duke University Chapel. I belatedly noted that none of these seventy-five years of sermons looked anything like the PowerPoint Preaching that I was now hearing everywhere. I have just read through a stack of Rick Warren's sermons. They are all, "How to Get More out of Worship," "The Way to Joy in Your Life," and, of course, "Purposeful Living." Warren majors in minor, abstract, general propositions such as "Five Ways to Get into God's Word." (A sermon that begins with "Last Sunday we said you need five things. You need people to live with, you need principles to live by, you need a profession to live out, you need power to live on, and you need purpose to live for."

Note the conspicuous absence of "God" from the list. God is apparently unnecessary when you have got the right list of principles.) Rick has succeeded in doing what no preacher in the Bible—much less preacher Jesus—has ever done: reduce the vast, bubbling mystery of biblical faith to a platitudinous slogan fit for a bumper sticker.

What we're seeing here is a curious Evangelical embrace of the old, now discredited, liberal attempt to reduce the Christian faith to its "essence," or its "essentials," reframing the historical, narrative Christian faith as a matter of abstract propositions and helpful ideas.[38] Marcus Borg does this, one more time, in his *Heart of Christianity*. The motivation for such reductionism is always apologetics. Borg says that he writes because "there are no serious intellectual obstacles to being a Christian. There is a way of seeing Christianity that makes persuasive and compelling sense of life in the broadest sense."[39] There you have it. If you look at Christianity through the lens that is given to you by late, capitalistic, market-driven, autonomous individual liberalism and if you reduce the faith to some generality that makes "sense of life in the broadest sense," then, wonder of wonders, no intellectual obstacle.

Marcus is perilously close to Rick's introduction to *The Purpose Driven Life*:

> This is more than a book; it is a guide to a 40-day spiritual journey that will enable you to discover the answer to life's most important question: What on earth am I here for? By the end of this journey you will know God's purpose for your life and will understand the big picture—how all the pieces of your life fit together. Having this perspective will reduce your stress, simplify your decisions, increase your satisfaction, and most important, prepare you for eternity.[40]

As preacher I breathlessly announce that at last I have found the key, the hidden *gnosis*, the true essence that will make Jesus more accessible to your ways of thinking without conversion of your ways of thinking. Rather than what you know being a gift of God (revelation), it's your personal epistemological achievement.

This appears to be the major motivation behind PowerPoint Preaching. Even though much of this is done by alleged evangelicals (like Rick), it is capitulation to the old liberal project. The gospel is advocated on the basis of its utility in effecting desired outcomes and goods that are neither internal to nor promised by the gospel. The wild scriptural narrative of creation and redemption into which we are to be inculcated by preaching is reduced to a more acceptable and manageable message. The gospel is truncated to fit the dominant cultural stories of who we are apart from being addressed by God.

The modern, essentially atheistic mentality despises mystery and considers enchantment and befuddlement an affront to its democratic right to know (and then to use) everything for purposes of individual fulfillment. The flattened mind loves lists, labels, solutions, sweeping propositions and practical principles. Vast, cosmic claims of the gospel are reduced to an answer to a question that, though it consumes contemporary North Americans, is hardly ever found in the Scripture: *what's in it for me?* The sovereign, free story of *God with us* is condensed to what can easily be managed, controlled, contained, and stabilized by me. Technopoly[41] deludes us into thinking that there is a tool for everything, including preaching, if we can find it and buy into it.

Limiting our preaching to immediate, practical impact and instant, quantifiable results prohibits preaching from being uniquely biblical. PowerPoint Preaching pushes for a selection of timeless *general principles*—rather than relationship with a complex *person* who is on the move, moving through time, our time, yet not bound by our time, not bound even to our wise general principles.

As Bonhoeffer noted, preaching is where Jesus Christ takes up room, where he deems to make himself available to the church. In Christ, God's Word became a person before God's words became a book. Preaching doesn't merely describe Christ, or offer some accurate ideas about Christ, or suggest some principles derived from Christ but is Christ's self-appointed medium of presence.

The proclaimed word has its origin in the incarnation of Jesus Christ. It neither originates from truth once perceived nor from personal experience. It is not the reproduction of a specific set of feelings. The proclaimed word is the incarnate Christ himself, the thing itself. The preached Christ is both the Historical One and the Present One. The proclaimed word is not a medium of expression for something else, something that lies behind it, but rather is the Christ himself walking through his congregation as the word.[42]

Augustine (in *De Doctrina Christiana*) observed that in the gospels Jesus is curiously depicted as always on a journey, always in movement where there is a not-too-soon determination of where we are headed with him. So many of the elements required to listen to a sermon—patience, time, a willingness to be confused by the other, risk of conversion into the other's world, respect for the integrity of the other—are precisely the skills required for friendship. Because of Scripture, the goal of truly biblical preaching is personal and relational rather than a set of manageable abstract propositions on a screen. It is more a matter of friendship than of intellectual understanding. The gospel is meant for embodied performance, not mere cognition. To paraphrase Stanley Hauerwas: if you can find a set of propositions that can give purpose to your life, go worship them rather than risking assault by this speaking, relentlessly demanding Jew from Nazareth.

No wonder PowerPoint Preaching is popular with us North Americans. It flatters my ego to be told, in effect, "Now here are some common sense principles that you, as a thinking, sensitive, empowered, self-sufficient modern person, will recognize as eternally useful." I then am invited by the preacher to pick and choose the principles that make sense to me. Rather than be coaxed into an alien story, or seduced into a new world, rather than hear a word that is not self-derived and not self-controlled, the preacher puts me in the driver's seat as the one who manages communication. This confirms my impression, engendered in me by a consumer culture, that religion is just another technique for getting what I want rather than a means of getting what God wants.

Preaching is thereby construed primarily as a product to be consumed. Through the adept presentation of information by rhetorical procedure, formulaic technique, and instrumental concern we get what the preacher judges to be "relevant" or "effective." Packaging is everything, and the best PowerPoint preacher is the one who cuts through all that irrelevant, archaic scriptural packaging and pointless, unprincipled biblical diversions, boiling everything down to *the message*: a set of abstract propositions and practical advice detached from the church that makes gospel propositions or advice work.[43] The goal of preaching becomes motivation of the listener, who exclaims, "I got it!" The result is almost unavoidably a gospel that is privatized, trivialized, and reduced to a memo that everyone can "get" without moral transformation or inculcation into a community that has, as one of its major tasks, our indoctrination into the rigors of faithful Christian listening (that is, prayer).[44] In orthodox Christian faith, the "message" is a Messenger. Therefore, most of us find that the gospel is more a matter of "it got me" than "I got it."

PowerPoint Preaching is often pushed as truly evangelistic preaching. As a preacher I am told that this method reassures anxious listeners—particularly the uninitiated listeners—providing them with a sense of intellectual certainty. "I got it," they murmur appreciatively on their way out of church. That is, they got a specific technique to take home and utilize in getting whatever they happen to want rather than Jesus. Thereby the embodied gospel is disembodied, abstracted from the story of the God who has, in Jesus Christ, "got" us. Preaching becomes subservient to the "real world" (that is, the governmentally sanctioned, officially defined world without God) of the omnivorous and always needy, modern consumer.

It's user-friendly Christianity as the triumph of the market. The congregation becomes another vendor of a "meaningful life" to individuals who come in, give a listen, take what techniques they can use, and then go home and have lunch with a minimum of fuss and bother.[45] A primary way that the reigning order protects itself from the cosmic, imperialistic claims of the gospel is to marginalize religion, making it a purely personal matter of individual choice. We continue under the illusion that we are free to decide and to choose which principles we serve without ever noticing our enslavement to the one principle that holds us captive: in order to have a life in capitalism, we are fated to decide and to choose which life we shall have.

More to the point of my central argument, PowerPoint Preaching also signifies an accommodation of Christian, eschatological time to pagan, Constantinian time. The vital, constantly moving, free Christian faith is stabilized into a set of eternal, universal, commonsensical, useful principles that appear normal to the average, thinking North American. We can attain understanding of a set of Christian ideas without having to have a Christ who enables the understanding of his ideas.

Christians believe there is no communication between *is* and *God* until God takes time. Therefore, preaching is not about the skillful application of technique and technology through PowerPoint. Faithful preaching is inherently eschatological in its refusal to capitulate to flat, godless time. Preaching is a form of prayer in which preacher and congregation show their utter dependence upon God to enter time, seize time, and speak—now. Therefore, faithful preaching is defiant and politically contentious in its attempt to make room for God to interrupt and wreak havoc with Caesar's determination to have the last word on this age.

As Isaiah says, "The grass withers, the flower fades," everything dissipates. We preachers can take heart in the reality that only one thing is eternal: "the word of our God will stand forever" (Isa 40:8). For the preacher, only one thing is eternal—the living word of a living God. To preach as a Christian is to claim *real presence*. Jesus was not a new idea. He was a new presence, a speaking, revealing presence. It was New Creation, not as mere renovation or extension of the old creation. The Galileans thought they heard a new teaching by Jesus (Mark 1:27) and the Athenians thought they heard, in Paul's address, something new (Acts 17:19). In a profound, yet inchoate way, they were right. A new One had come on the scene (Eph 2:15; Col 3:10), genuinely new. That "new [thing]" foretold by Isaiah (Isa 48:6), the "new heaven and new earth" of Revelation 21:1 was here, in God. Those who thought old wine is better than new (Luke 5:39) were wrong. There's a new commandment in town (John 13:34). "Behold I make all things new," says the one who now, after Resurrection, rules (Rev 21:5 KJV).

Humor is thus a part of Easter because, as is in so many good jokes, humor gives us a temporary escape from the bounds of history. In a joke, things don't end as they usually do in life. We are surprised. We smile. There is room, God-granted space between the determinations of history and time as God is making time God's.[46] We are not to take the present too seriously, as if now is all there is that is going on in the world. Thus the saints once spoke of Easter as the great joke God played on the devil.

We are ultimately hopeful and humorous about the future because we already have seen the future. The One who is, and is yet to come, is also the one who has come. This new is not merely some future hope but is already present as event, as newly enacted here and now. That's what "kingdom of God is at hand" meant in the preaching of Jesus. In preaching, Jesus took time for us. In Easter, that which was concealed in the earthly life of Jesus was revealed, became present to us, now. That which was from before the foundation of the world (John 1) became real, now, whenever the Risen Christ slipped through locked doors and was present (John 20). We who were "once . . . far off" have "now . . . been brought near" (Eph 2:13). Whenever this story is preached, it is effected. Whenever anybody hears anything in a sermon, the kingdom of God has come near, now, death's grip on the world is broken—it's Easter all over again.

Surely that's why, though John could have written in his Gospel enough words about Jesus to fill more books than the world could contain, John wrote just these words that we might come to believe that Jesus is Messiah, Son of God, that we might have life here, now in his name (John 20:31). Jesus preached, "the time is fulfilled, and the kingdom of God has come near" (Mark 1:15) and Galatians 4:4 depicts Christ's birth as when "the time had fully come." "Behold, now is the acceptable time; behold, now is the day of salvation" (2 Cor 6:2 KJV).

Ancient words, spoken then, spoken to them, remembered, recollected from the past so that Christ might be present to us—it's a move that happens all the time in preaching.

A Sermon: It's about Time

Then he told this parable: "A man had a fig tree planted in his vineyard; and he came looking for fruit on it and found none. So he said to the gardener, 'See here! For three years I have come looking for fruit on this fig tree, and still I find none. Cut it down! Why should it be wasting the soil?' He replied, 'Sir, let it alone for one more year, until I dig around it and put manure on it. If it bears fruit next year, well and good; but if not, you can cut it down.'" (Luke 13:6-9)

They say that in Martin Luther's class on Genesis, a smart aleck student asked, "Dr. Luther, since you know so much about the book of Genesis, tell us: what was God doing all that time before God created the world?"

Luther, not one to be one-upped by a smart-mouthed seminarian, replied, "What was God doing before God created the world? God was gathering sticks to make a switch to beat the hell out of people like you who ask such dumb questions!"

But seriously, what was God doing all that time? It's not a dumb question. What was there for God to do before God did for us? What did God think about before God thought about you and me?

And in the exodus, it was wonderful when God finally came down and heard the cry of the Hebrew slaves. But some of the glory of the exodus fades when one realizes that they had been crying in slavery *for 430 years!* Why did God wait 430 years before liberating the Hebrew children?

The Bible has been called the book of the "mighty acts of God." But according to my reckoning, the Bible covers well over two thousand years of history—God's history. True, there are really impressive, though occasional, actions by God. But there are also these large gaps when God doesn't say or do anything. John Calvin said that if God would withdraw his beneficent hand from Creation for even an instant, everything would fall apart, collapse into chaos, and be nothing. But there are some rather

21

long periods of time, if you read between the lines of Scripture, when God doesn't seem to do anything, or at least anything worth writing down in the book of Numbers.

Almost everything we know about Jesus takes place in less than a three-year span after he was thirty. What was Jesus doing all that time before he was thirty? Most of us regard our childhood, youth, and young adulthood as the most formative and among the most important times of our lives. Why were those years so uneventful for Jesus? All the way between kindergarten and college graduation, one would have thought Jesus might have done something memorable during all those years. But no, nothing noteworthy.

In John's Gospel, Mary and Martha send Jesus the urgent plea, "Lazarus, our brother whom you love, is ill. Come quick!" (John 11:3, author's paraphrase). Friend Lazarus is near death. Two terrified sisters wait anxiously.

John says that Jesus waited *three more days* before setting out for Bethany. Why? No reason is given. Doesn't say that Jesus was otherwise engaged, busy with more pressing work. Just says he hung around where he was for three days. Of course, by the time Jesus got to Bethany, Lazarus was dead, the funeral was over, he was entombed, and as Martha later told Jesus (in the old Authorized Version) "by this time he stinketh."

Why did Jesus wait three days before going to Lazarus's aid? Jesus tells Martha, when she chides him for taking his own sweet time to get to Bethany, to pipe down because this was all "for the glory of God." What's the "glory" in taking three days to respond to someone in such urgent need?

Saint Augustine, in thinking about time, says that God doesn't count time as we count time. I'll say.

Paul tells his churches, "Don't marry! Don't worry about being slaves! Don't bother about persecution by the government! It will all be over soon. The Lord is coming—sometime."

Some of his churches wrote to Paul saying, "OK. We're hurting. It's been decades. We're still waiting! Any word on when you expect Jesus?"

And 2 Peter answers, "Er, uh, don't you know that with the Lord, one day is like a thousand of our years? What seems like a long time to you is no time at all to an eternal God" (2 Pet 3:8, author's paraphrase).

Nice try, 2 Peter. I've heard of procrastination, but really!

Ecclesiastes eloquently proclaims that there is a time to be born and a time to die, a time to make peace and a time to make war, a time to laugh and a time to cry. For everything under heaven there is just the right time. Beautiful thought.

But then Ecclesiastes follows with a not-so-beautiful thought: *and only God knows when that right time is!* (Eccl 2:10-12).

There is just the right time for this, and the right time for that, but you'll never know the time! God just doesn't do time the way we keep time.

Thus this gospel. Jesus tells a story about a woefully unproductive fig tree that's wasted a lot of time. Let me put the story of the barren fig tree in context. Luke's chapter 13 opens with focus on time (*kairos*). We live in a lousy time, judging by the newspapers. A couple of horrible contemporary tragedies are put before Jesus.

"Jesus, did you hear about those poor people on whom the tower fell during the earthquake? What did they do to be in the wrong place at the wrong time?

"And did you read about the poor Galileans who were murdered by Pilate when they were just trying faithfully to worship God? What did they do to deserve this? Why didn't God intervene and protect these martyrs? Where was God at the time when they were getting their throats slit?"

Jesus cryptically responds by not answering their questions but by saying, "I tell you, if you don't repent, you will likewise perish." Not the most pastoral of responses, I'd say. Here are two tragedies, one caused by natural evil and the other by political evil, and Jesus responds by judgmental demands for repentance from those who dare to ask, "Where is God now? Why doesn't God come, now?"

It's right then that Jesus tells the story about the poorly producing fig tree. Three years, no figs. Fig trees should bear every year. And in Judea, fig trees even bear fruit twice every year. But this tree has never borne fruit.

"Cut it down!" says the owner. Time's up.

But a servant pleads, "Master, let it alone [Greek: *aphes*, which also can mean 'forgive it']. I'll dig around it, pile manure [Greek: *koprion*, which also means 'dung,' 'feces,' or worse] on it, and then let's see what happens and you can do as you please."

Three years is a long time to wait for fruit, a long time to be patient with such a worthless tree in a place where land is at a premium. And still the servant begs for more time for the tree.

There are times, when we're waiting on God to do something for us, when (sad to say) God seems to take forever.

*And there are times when God is waiting on us to do something for God, when (thank God) God seems to **give** forever.*

"Lord make haste to save us!" cry the psalmists (Pss 22:19; 31:22; 40:13; 70:1). In my experience, rarely does God make hurry. And that's hard, especially when you are suffering, or needing an answer, or waiting for deliverance. God didn't run to hold back that falling tower or hasten to stop the murderous wrath of Pilate. God didn't scurry to raise Lazarus or hasten to free the Hebrew slaves. In such times, God seems so slow.

And sometimes divine tardiness is a blessing. Jesus tells a story about a tree that, in all justice, ought to be cut down.[47] Yet a servant pleads, "Master, give it some more time." And that's grace, especially when you have yet to bear the good fruit that God expects from you, or when you have yet to take root, or when you have not yet come to blossom into what you were created to be. In such times, God's delay is God's gift. There's still time.

I know a woman who, after her diagnosis of cancer, prayed twice every day for God to heal her. A year later, as she entered her third round of chemotherapy, she said, "Well, it looks like once again, God isn't on my schedule. I guess God's decided to heal me at some other place, in some other time." She had been given a level of faith, in that time, I have yet to reach.

A therapist once told me that, in therapy, the greatest challenge is to offer help at the right time. "People's problems must be allowed to ripen," she explained. "The premature offer of a solution to their problem will not be received. The therapist must be patient, must allow the client to talk, and talk, and wait and wait for just the right time." Aristotle said that, in telling someone the truth, the trick was to tell that person the truth at the right time. Maybe God knows enough about us not to rush. Maybe.

Maybe Jesus didn't drop everything and rush to the bedside of Lazarus because Jesus isn't jerked around by what jerks us. Maybe we are not at the center of God's time. We think of time in terms of what God needs to do for us. Maybe God looks at our time as that time we are given to do what needs doing for God. And, according to the parable, there's still time.

When old atheist Malcolm Muggeridge wrote his spiritual autobiography about his late-in-life conversion to Christ, he called it, *Chronicles of Wasted Time*.

One of the greatest challenges of loving God is to permit God to keep God's own good time. We have faith that God will come to us, will heal us, will save us—but not always on our schedule, not always on our time. Will you praise God, even when God doesn't run to you?

I'll tell you, as your preacher. One of the toughest tasks of being a preacher is allowing the Holy Spirit to enter, to enlighten, and to speak to my listeners—when and where the Holy Spirit chooses. Believe it or not, I've worked hard on this sermon. I've carefully crafted what I want to say to you so as to communicate with you here, now, without fail.

But I've been preaching long enough to know that no matter what I preach, it isn't a sermon, it isn't God's word for the congregation unless and until the Holy Spirit descends and enables them to hear. It's not a sermon until God says it's a sermon. I want that time of revelation to be now, right now, while I'm talking. But sometimes I can tell, just by looking at the congregation's faces that once again, God is taking God's own sweet time with my sermon!

Jesus tells this story of the barren fig tree on his way to Jerusalem. He is not at his destination. He is on the way. At the end, there will be judgment. For now, there is still time. Jesus tells this story to me and to you who are not at our destination. We are here today, still on our life's way. By the pleading of the servant, by God's grace, for you and for me, there is still time.

Is this a story about judgment ("Cut it down!") or about grace ("Give it more time!")? I suppose that the answer to that lies in what time it is in your life related to God's own good time.

There will be judgment, accounting, a day when fruitfulness will be examined ("Cut it down!") *and* there is still time ("Give it more time!"). Justice is here depicted as accounting for fruitfulness; mercy is here depicted as time. There shall be a time when time's up. And there is, by God's grace, still time.

Perhaps it's because of my advanced age (I've clearly got more yesterdays on my account than tomorrows), but I find that I wake up each morning surprised, grateful even, just to be waking up in the morning! I find myself saying to myself, "So. You have one more day. What a surprise. What a gift. So, what will I do with today?" The time before me is both a gift and an assignment, grace and judgment. What will we do, what will God do, with the time?

A man in my congregation had dangerous open heart surgery. He was told by the doctor he had no more than a fifty-fifty chance of survival during the surgery. But he did survive. When I visited him afterwards, I said, "You did survive after all! Isn't that wonderful?"

He said, "No, preacher, I didn't survive. I did more than survive; I was born again. I'm not the same person I have been for the past fifty years. I've been given a second chance and I'm going to be different, better than before." His postoperative time was for him a time of both judgment and grace.

The servant says to the master, "Let me dig around the roots, turn up the soil, disrupt the fig tree, pile some smelly manure on it, and let's see if the dung does the trick." Fig trees require almost no special cultivation. This is extraordinary horticulture. So maybe in those times when you think your time has turned terrible—and the *koprion* is getting deep— maybe you are being cultivated for greater fruitfulness. The same servant who pled for more time is the friend who is piling on the *koprion,* using the time to produce more fruit. Maybe.

Jesus' parable is a play in two acts: (1) "Cut it down!" then (2) "Give it time!" I guess that means that we're now living out the third act. How long did the master wait? Surely his patience is not forever. Did the dung do it? Was there ever fruit? We don't know because, as in so many of Jesus' parables, this one doesn't have an ending. Maybe that's because God is still working on the ending, and so are we. By God's grace we're given time to finish the story.

Are you willing, in your heartache and struggles, for God to take time from you, or to take time for you or, or to give time to you? Are you able, in the time that God gives you, to take time for God?

The gospel, good news for this Sunday in Ordinary Time: *there's still time.*

CHAPTER TWO

TIME'S THIEF

Kurt Vonnegut said that most good stories occur when a character gets "unstuck in time."[1] Lives become interesting only when, in tragedy or in comedy, the time of our lives is disrupted, becomes unstuck. Horror novelist Stephen King, out for a jog one morning, was hit by a speeding van. He spent weeks in the hospital, fighting for his life, in terrible pain. In an interview with NPR's Terry Gross, King admitted that the accident changed his life and afterward he had written some of his best novels.[2]

"Still, if someone had given me the choice of retiring peacefully to New England," said King, "or getting hit by a van and writing two or three more good books, I would have chosen retirement in a heartbeat." Listening to that interview, I muttered, "In my religion, that speeding, disrupting, homicidal van is sometimes named 'God.'"

What is God like? Jesus replies: a homeowner sleeps, secure in his ownership (Luke 12:39). During the night, he awakes in horror; a thief has broken into his home and ripped off everything. He dearly wishes that he had known that the time of his dormancy would be the time of a robbery, but he didn't. Now he's the loser. Jesus warns that each of us should live as if we were about to get ripped off by God. Losers, wake up!

I'll grant that Jesus' parable is not the most flattering image of God. God's a thief who breaks in and rips you off?

Jesus, teller of this outrageous tale, incarnates the thief who shatters the illusion of time's normalcy. Jesus strides in and takes time.[3] What's "new" in Jesus is the "now" of Jesus. Others had talked "kingdom of God." (Luke, for instance, tirelessly reiterates that Jesus Christ is not new: Christ is the fulfillment of the ancient promises of God to Israel.) It took Jesus to preach that the "kingdom of God *has come near*" (Luke 10:9). What was new is that Jesus said that the day of the Lord is *now*. He met our apocalyptic expectation with his earth-shaking presence. Trouble is, once apocalyptic expectation became messianic reality—present—we discovered that this was not at all the presence we thought we were awaiting. We looked at Jesus and said, "Please, not so near, not so excruciatingly present, not in this place, not in this Jew. Not in any Jew, in fact."

"The Kingdom of God has come near" is ambiguous news. Jesus discovered that in the congregational reaction to his first sermon in Nazareth (Luke 4). Things went OK as he read the poetic words of Isaiah. Then Jesus had the gall to announce, "*Today* these past words are now (fulfilled) in your hearing," and church was out. It was the nearness, the "nowness" that caused crisis and demanded change, now. Salvation is always easier when it is delayed, future and therefore harmless. Here, now is a demanding gift. In a threatening tone of voice Paul preached, "Now is the day of salvation" (2 Cor 6:2).

Yet here's the paradox. It was not only that Jesus was God present, here, now. It was also that God was in *Jesus Christ* reconciling the world to himself (2 Cor 5:19). In Jesus, we met the God whom we had not known, did not want to know. God *pro nobis*, for us, tends always to be perceived as the God *anti nobis*, the God against us. God is hidden precisely in God's availability to the world. In Jesus "incarnation" was not only in flesh but also in time. And when our time is commandeered by *that* particular God, well, we get nervous and our defenses against God are activated.[4] Some of us wanted to see God but were disappointed that God was in Jesus of Nazareth, now, here.

A favorite way of defending ourselves against the challenge of Jesus' immanence ("Today . . . fulfilled.") is through history, the claim that our problem with God is historical and that the way to hear Scripture is through the help of historians.[5] Trouble is, when we say "history" we demonstrate our attenuated historical imagination in which time is thought to be a more or less uniform, coherent sequence of events.

Even though modernity did not invent the notion of cause-effect—do this, you will almost always get that—modernity is based to a great degree on the notion that there is only one efficient cause for every effect and that efficient cause is not God. Hume noted that the great goal of modern thinking was sequential predictability, the ability to isolate cause so that one could predict effect. The invention and ubiquity of the clock in modernity gives the illusion of time's uniformity, measurability, and linear progression. The clock makes time fleeting, incessant, and ultimately irretrievable. In modernity, we're always losing time, killing time, and wasting time because we've lost the means to retrieve time past or live into the future. Time without God is denuded, impoverished time, time without meaning. Boredom plagues modern people because we've robbed time of any agency other than our own actions, producing lots of empty, boring time with few surprises.[6]

God, the maker of history, is driven out of time by the device of modern history. The historian explains the course of history, its causes and their effects, without reference to God, thus making history an exclusively human product.[7]

"Everything is a question of chronology,"[8] says Proust, the greatest artistic neurasthenic of all time. The Greeks tried to overcome time through imagining divinity as that which lacks all temporal boundaries. Greek gods transcend death by their immunity to the ravages of time. Christians see things differently. The triune God transcends death by triumphing over it, by the Son's dying in time and by the Father's raising him up in the power of the Holy Spirit for all time. The Greeks saw divinities as serene, ideal, and only occasionally, capriciously descending from Parnassus to become briefly involved in the grubby vicissitudes of human history. The resurrection narratives depict a God who is constantly on the move, energetic, revealing here, now. The Greeks predicated a quiet serenity at the ultimate heart of all things. Easter stories depict a God who refuses to stop talking and cease walking. Here is a God who takes time, not to be immune from time's vicissitudes, but to be eternally faithful in time. "Your faithfulness endures to all generations . . ." (Ps 119:90). In every generation God keeps rising up and defeating time in order to keep God's commitments in time, in order to keep talking, keep relating. Thus Easter brings us to the heart of Christian preaching and life with a God in time who refuses to be silent. The Easter mandate is the vocative, "Go! Tell!"

Again, Bonhoeffer states:

> The proclaimed word is the incarnate Christ himself . . . the thing itself.
> The preached Christ is both the Historical One and the Present One.
> . . . The proclaimed word is not a medium of expression for something
> else, something which lies behind it, but rather is the Christ himself
> walking through his congregation as the word.[9]

I'm saying that preachers "make it new" by "making it now," if we are to preach like Jesus. Preaching like Jesus is preaching Jesus. All preaching is Easter preaching, dependent upon the truth of resurrection to make it work. To preach in any time is to expect immanence, to make an eschatological claim that time between us and God has been, is being, will be bridged by God in Christ.

True, the Kingdom is "near" but not fully "now." Preaching works that space between redemption accomplished and redemption still being finished. Preaching Christ is always a proleptic endeavor—talk about something that has already occurred yet is still to occur, is now occurring. As Barth says, our salvation in Christ is an "intrinsically perfect work" (in cross and resurrection, redemption is accomplished; nothing else is needed) and yet that work "is still moving toward its consummation."[10] Our redemption is already accomplished in eternity, from the beginning of time, into all time. Thus when we experience redemption, realize our salvation, acknowledge who God is and what God has done for us, we are simply beholding variations of one and the same event. Barth even said that, as we regard time from the view of Scripture, "eternity comes first and then time, and therefore the future comes first and then the present."[11] We literally don't know what time it is now until eternity is revealed to us, along with the future. Only then do we know what time it is. First eternity, then the present. Jesus Christ the same yesterday and tomorrow becomes the same Jesus Christ today.

The Holy Spirit contemporizes, reveals, and imparts our redemption here and now. Sadly for us preachers, the Holy Spirit seems to be the most neglected person of the Trinity in contemporary theology. We preachers need a robust conviction of the Holy Spirit's work because we, unlike most academic interpreters of the Christian faith or of Scripture, must stand up and speak a word to God's people, here, now. The Holy Spirit is the power of God, empowering humanity to know God. The Holy Spirit is God's agency in preaching, that which makes a sermon work.

The Holy Spirit is not some impersonal force, not some vague sense, but rather has a distinct personality, as portrayed in Scripture. I would characterize that personality as dynamic, difficult, destructive, life-giving, creative but disruptively creative (Genesis 1; Acts 2). In the power of the Holy Spirit Jesus told us to pray for the coming of God's reign and to not lose heart (Matt 6:10). But not because God was holding something back. It was now but not yet. It is not fully here, not only because a nonviolent God refuses to force or to coerce that reign upon us. (We may still turn away and reject, refuse, and decline.) Yet the Kingdom also seemed distant, even as Jesus stood beside us, because it was *Jesus* who stood beside us. The nearness of the Kingdom, in Jesus, gave us a close look into what God's kingdom was really like. Jesus made us pray, "Thy Kingdom come, thy will be done on earth as it is in heaven," now, here as it will be then, there.

It was much easier for us to think about God's will being fulfilled somewhere else at a time other than now. Jesus violated the comfort of our historical postponement of God's time by his daring assertion that the reign of God is now. Yet he also violated the comfort of any smug sense of immanence by standing near us as the stranger whom we did not expect. The narratives of Jesus' resurrection teach us what we might reasonably expect from a living God. God is whoever raised Jesus Christ from the dead.[12]

Nineteenth-century historian Adolf von Harnack wrote, "No religion gains anything through time, it only loses." This provided the mandate for the historian to recover as much as possible from the past in order to make Christianity relevant. All of this made perfect sense considered apart from the resurrection and the gift of the Holy Spirit. Death gets everything, except what the historian can retrieve.

Yet if we believe in the resurrection, time must be reconsidered. Because of resurrection, and the activity of the Holy Spirit, we have more time left with God in the future than in the past.[13] Although the mighty acts of God in the past (Scripture) are impressive, some of God's most interesting work may yet be before us. Who knows what the Holy Spirit will be up to next? We believe that time's dominance (death) has been broken. So why would we turn to the historians for help with revelation of God after the resurrection?[14]

In 1908 Ernst Troeltsch, professor of systematic theology at Heidelberg, wrote an assessment of theology in Germany during the previous half century. Among Troeltsch's contentions was that theological work must be a cultural synthesis that meets the religious needs of an age. Historical study of Christianity that recovered the essence of the faith, its relevant content for our culture, is the only way for Christianity to survive in the brave new world of modern Germany. A young pastor in Switzerland, Karl Barth, heard Troeltsch's lecture in 1910. After hearing the lecture, Barth wrote that he had "the dark foreboding that it had become impossible to advance any farther in the Dead-end street where [theologians] were strolling in relative comfort."[15] Why this gloomy assessment of Troeltsch? Barth said that it was "impossible for a historian as such to do justice to Christianity"[16] Human methods (like history) can never construct a living God, at best only producing, in Kierkegaard's contemptuous phrase, "disciples at second hand."[17]

Barth was indebted to the great anti-theologian, Franz Overbeck (1837–1905) for his low regard of the helpfulness of historiography for Christianity. Overbeck said that the resurrected Christ is complete contradiction rather than continuity with the old world. (For example, Overbeck made much of the fact that the resurrection sounded the death knell for slavery in the Roman Empire. After Easter, it was a whole new world.) Most contemporary "theology"—in its degraded synthesis of ancient and modern, with modern culture calling the shots—was condemned by Overbeck as a complete contradiction of Christianity's most basic affirmation (the resurrection). If Jesus has been raised from the dead, then "Christian religion"—as a mix of the culture of the world as it was with bits and pieces of Christian insight that do not threaten the order of this age—is a travesty.[18] "Time" as understood after the resurrection has little in common with "time" as historians continue to use the term.

Karl Barth was deeply influenced by Overbeck's unmasking of the fraud of contemporary, liberal German theology—in attempting to make Christianity "relevant" to the modern age, theologians had only succeeded in trimming down cosmic Christian claims to unthreatening moral platitudes. I also believe that Barth came to this realization through his own frustration with the task of preaching in his early attempts to preach at Safenwil. Barth discovered that no preacher can make God real to anybody, no matter how hard the preacher tries. Preaching is impossible. Our human analogies fail when speaking about God, including such analogies as *eternal* and *historical*. The church has the assigned task to signify the gospel, but the church has not the power to make the gospel significant.

If God is God, then only God can determine when God will speak through what we preachers say or do. We are unable, through our meager human means, to conjure up the Holy Spirit. Augustine asserted that preaching was to instruct, to move, and to delight, but Barth says that we can't do any of that. Theology is the description of "an embarrassment," in that we are called to speak God's word and yet we are unable to speak God's word.[19] Only God can speak of God. Only God can preach. Only God can make God's word relevant.

In Jesus Christ, the reign of God is present—not as a progressive, gradual result of astute thinking or hard work, not as the result of quiet, introspective centering and spiritual exercises—but rather as unexpected interruption, intervention, new beginning, new creation, the eschatological end of history, the gift of the Holy Spirit that we did not want. Now.[20] This is a major reason why the Christian faith cannot be subjected to time, can neither be reduced to history nor apprehended by the historical. It is also the major reason why the most traumatic thing that can happen to anybody is baptism.

This more-than-the-historical quality of the faith presents Christianity with a great challenge because modernity made history humanity's basic mode of existence. Karl Barth said that modernity had made time into "absolute time," the one, irrevocable "absolute reality" in which we are trapped and from which there is no escape. People can think, plan, project, and create, but nobody can escape the ravages of time. All cheerful humanistic assessments of humanity wilt before omnivorous death, death that is the human experience of the passage of time. This is the chronological prison in which we live. We think that we are free, that our actions can somehow stay the constant march of time, yet we live enclosed within "these walls."[21]

Barth said that this was thinking about "time without God"[22] in which time itself takes on divine-like characteristics, in which time becomes absolute, omnipotent, and indefatigable. Most godless attempts to think about time make time into "a God called Chronos."[23] Attempts to speak about "infinity," or the divine as infinite, said Barth, are akin to the Greek (pagan) attempt to make time into a god. In the modern period, a variation of this pagan project is the "idea of endless progress."[24] We haven't said the God of the Old and New Testaments when we say "Infinite One." When God reveals God's self by entering time, God thereby defeats the idea of infinity. Barth said that by clinging to ideas of the possibility of infinity or progress we delude ourselves about the nature of time.

For Barth, "absolute time" is time separated from God, an attempt to fit God into the confines of our temporal domain. "History" has become the study of human actions and their results, the study of humanity without reference to humanity's relation to God. History has become the fantasy of those who attempt to live in the temporal as if that were God. Barth said that abstract, absolute thinking about time "apart from the will and Word and work of God is itself the product of the perverted and sinful thinking of man, one of the manifestations of human pride."[25]

We therefore attempt to make Jesus a historical datum. We do research and investigation on Jesus, using history as a method of retrieval of that which is not ours, not of our time, something distant and removed from us. This historicism is a denial of our time as the time claimed by God. Ensconced in imperial Rome, Caesar thought he was making history. Then Jesus of Nazareth stole it.

Failing at historical retrieval, unable to figure out the truth of the past, sometimes we flee the present into the future. Tomorrow will be better. We write science fiction. Eventually we find that we are unable to live backwards into the past or to project ourselves realistically into the future. In truth, we are lonely. Frantically hunting for a time that has meaning for us, the hunter becomes the hunted.[26] Barth says that we Westerners react to this situation with endless striving and "conscientious work" while Easterners react with "resignation," both the result of making time "absolute time."[27] A longing for infinity robs us of real time here and now. Infinity is a delusion. In attempting to make time our own, without God, we no longer have time.[28]

Infinity is vacant, lonely, endless time, time without God. *There will always be tomorrow* is a lie. *Eternity* is time with God. God doesn't just give us time (time between the resurrection of Jesus and final consummation of Creation); God takes time.[29] If we believe that God reveals God's self to us, then we believe that God has taken time for us.[30] God has determined, in Jesus Christ, not to be eternal without us. God takes time *pro nobis*. The Old and New Testaments, in the form of their presentation of Christ—not in eternal concepts or principles but in a story that, like any story, moves through time with beginning, middle, and end—is the narration of a history, something that occurs in time. God is not made over time, but God makes time. We therefore do not know what time it is until it is revealed what God is doing in time.

To know that we are bounded, limited creatures, that we are finite not infinite, mortal not immortal, to know that, really to know that, that's news. We believe, with Genesis 3:19, that our lives are bounded by death. That this should come as news to us is sign of our sin.

And yet, with Acts 17:26, we believe that the limits of our lives—the *boundedness* of life as fixed by God—is also a gracious gift of God. Our time is restricted. This life is not fated to go on forever, one damned thing, or one blessed thing, after another. Our lives are bounded not just by death but by Providence, Presence.

How can such knowledge—our time is finite, bounded in death—be considered a gracious gift? This is an insight granted to those who know that our lives are bounded *by* God. Death is the great boundary of life and, in the resurrection of Jesus Christ, God is the great boundary of death. Death limits life, but on Easter God limited death. Only then death loses its quality as the great final fact, the dominator of every moment of life. In Easter, death stops seeming like judgment, a curse, the thief, the final enemy, and begins to appear as forgiveness, blessing, sometimes even friend. No stoic resignation, the stiff upper lip of the doomed, is now demanded. Rather, thanksgiving, rejoicing even, which is what Revelation says our future is like. The door that was shut to us in death swings open, not by our striving or our positive attitude but rather by God. That which heretofore was exclusively ending is—surprise— beginning. We are not just given more time (in my pastoral experience, few people who are near death want that). We are given more radiant time, more presence time, time more fully to be with God and God with us.

God takes time, our time, to be with us. There is nothing new in this world except the kingdom of God, the only true escape from the downward pull of history, the only real breakthrough from the facts of life (and death). Death now has no dominion. Easter is absolutely unexpected, inconceivable. It is something that comes down from heaven and breaks through everything that we think we have learned about life and the world. It is God's grand revolution in time but against time. Barth says that the kingdom of God, radiantly revealed in the Resurrection, makes all other revolutions that we think we've experienced in history and in time as "little revolutions."[31] As Barth said, in his work on Christian ethics, published posthumously, the kingdom of God is not just something new, it is *the* new, the only truly new thing we've seen since we are put together from dust, "it is the new thing *of God*."[32]

Barth's exegesis of Romans 4:23-25 ("Now it was not written for his sake alone, that he was reckoned unto [Abraham] but for our sake also, unto whom it shall be reckoned, who believe him that raised Jesus our Lord from the dead . . . and was raised for our justification," ASV) is instructive. In *Romans* Barth asks what on earth Abraham's history is supposed to mean for us? How could words that were written to Abraham be God's word to us?[33]

Barth answers that this is peculiar history in that it speaks to us. Throughout his *Church Dogmatics* Barth quite deliberately conflates the two German words for history *Geschichte* and *Historie*. *Historie* tends to be the more specialized term that originated in the nineteenth century for the academic discipline of historical study. For many, this means the uncovered "facts" of history, what "really happened" back then. This word is in contrast to *Geschichte,* which can mean everything from "report" to "tale" or "story." Barth does not accept the distinction as a serious one when reading the Bible. Whatever history might be able to verify and establish was, for Barth, "trivial." In Scripture, by work of the Holy Spirit, what the world regards as a long-dead *Historie* becomes our currently lived story.

The great sin of humanity (in regard to time) is to act as if we are in time without God, to act is if our past is our past by ourselves, as if our future and present is in our hands. People who live only for themselves, in time by themselves, are not fully human, for humanity (according to Barth) is relationship.[34] When, in listening to a sermon, the risen Christ comes to you, reaches out to you, stands with you, part of the thrill of that moment is the joy of being a human being fully alive to a relationship with God. Until Christ becomes alive to us, we are not alive. It is a similar dynamic whenever we are loved by another. We can't have the present except as a gift of the God who dares to be present with us in the present.

> This present day of ours is also a day of the living Jesus Christ. . . . It may well be a day when no moment passes in which death does not make . . . an . . . end of some human life. It may well be a day of the devil. . . . This is true. But it is not decisive. The decisive thing is that it is also a day of Jesus Christ, a day of His presence, life, activity and speech . . . a day of His coming again in the full sense of the word. . . . We are contemporaries of Jesus Christ and direct witnesses of His action, whether with closed or open or blinking eyes, whether actively or passively. More closely and properly than any other man . . . He is the neighbor . . . , the Good Samaritan for all of us. . . . Wittingly or unwittingly we are alongside and with Him. His today is really ours and ours His.[35]

Barth says that in the resurrection Jesus appeared breathtakingly "in the mode of God," that is, the risen Christ was God in that he was more clearly present as past, present, and future so that "no longer" and "not yet" don't apply to him.[36] He is simultaneously present in all three tenses. Even though Jesus was different in his past, he is the same Jesus Christ yesterday, today, and tomorrow. He is the one "who is and who was and who is to come" (Rev 1:8).[37]

God not only takes time, but God gives us time. We genuinely do have time. We have a present and a future because God gives it to us. When I take time to give someone else an hour of my time, that is one of my greatest gifts. I am literally giving them time, transforming their time by my willingness to enter their time and to allow them to enter mine.

Christians believe that something like that has happened in Jesus Christ.

Easter: He's Back

I recall a theologian who, though now mostly forgotten, had a big effect upon preaching in my misspent youth: Rudolf Bultmann. Time was a big issue for Bultmann, an agenda set by his teacher, Heidegger.[38] Bultmann, wonderfully adept in the literature of Israel, was fascinated that there is so little in Jesus' preaching that could be called "new." Bultmann correctly identified the imminence of the reign of God as that which Jesus preached. Yet Bultmann believed that Jesus' preaching of the imminent reign of God was a grand mistake. "The proclamation of the irruption of God's Reign was not fulfilled. Jesus' expectation of the near end of the world turned out to be an illusion."[39] Jesus died a frustrated prophet. Distinguishing between the "Jesus of history" (Jesus caught in time, an historical figure about which little can be retrieved) and the "Christ of faith" (Jesus raised into eternity, free of time, a metaphysical entity with little substance or content), Bultmann essentially denied the resurrection as having historical reality.

In order to retrieve some earthly relevance for the resurrected "Christ of faith," Bultmann then lapsed into an existentialist interpretation of the "reign of God" that enabled him to rescue some significance for the "now" of Christ by removing the kingdom of God from history and positing it in our modern subjectivity. The resurrection is the way that the risen Christ is to us now and the main means of that presence is in preaching. Jesus Christ has been raised into the kerygma, into preaching. Jesus Christ is now personal address (*Anrede*), strong demand (*Forderung*) that requires not our intellectual understanding but rather our full obedience. Jesus Christ is not simply more information; he is address that calls for decision. Though Bultmann spoke of the importance of a "decision" (without specifying much content in that decision), a sense of "crisis" occasioned by the preaching of Jesus, his existentialism forced him to honor the sovereign self of modernity, leaving it undisturbed by Jesus' eschatological disruption of history.[40] The self's awareness of the risen Christ is that which validates and certifies the risen Christ.

The need for Christian eschatology to submit to the demands of modernity was identified by Bultmann as *the* problem of Christian preaching. Bultmann felt that this biblical talk of a promised resurrection of the dead at the end of the world and the end to human history as we know it needed thoroughgoing demythologizing. He called for the translation of eschatological (that is, primitive) Jewish-Christian ideas of time into the existentialist time of modernity, thus to make Christianity relevant:

> Until we translate this gospel into a language that enlightened men today can understand, we are depriving ourselves of the very resources on which the continued success of our witness most certainly depends. . . . If the price of becoming a faithful follower of Jesus Christ is some form of self-destruction, whether of the body or of the mind—*sacrificium corporis, sacrificium intellectus* . . . [that] price must remain unpaid.[41]

Although Bultmann attempted to construe the Christian faith in a way that would not demand the "sacrifice of the intellect," he not only endangered the truthfulness of the gospel but also imperiled the gospel's timefulness.[42] The existential decision that is demanded by Christ becomes awfully thin and rather vague in Bultmann. The content of the "decision for Christ" is a "decision," though the ethical demands or the shape of that decision remain unspecified. Christ becomes a sort of Christ-symbol, timeless, above the tug and pull of earthly existence, a means of achieving inward detachment from the strain and stress of the world.[43]

The Gospels testify that Jesus was raised into time, our time. "He is risen!" the women first preached, running back from the tomb. He *is* risen. He not only is raised, but he also speaks for himself, now. He appears, shattering our normalcy. He identifies himself, quite specifically, as God, though not the God whom we expected. So the women preached not, "He is risen into his eternal self," but rather, "He's back."

Time's Invasion

In a sense, on Easter or any other high holy day, our challenge is the same as on any Sunday—belief not only that Jesus Christ is Lord, but that he is Lord *now* and all other lordlets are not. There is room for only one Lord on the throne. The reign of God has come near and that nearness, in space and time, has subversive implications, here, now. God takes up room among us as Lord, and thereby subverts, pushes aside competing rulers. When our preaching of the gospel is detached from visible, active obedience to the gospel here and now (that is, the church) and from the tense, expectant, disruptive power of God's future (that is, eschatology), our preaching wilts into some sort of report on a past event rather than, as it ought to be, proclamation of a divinely disruptive present reign. It is not only that God was in Christ reconciling the world to himself but that God was *in Christ*.

It is somewhat bemusing to note the plethora of modern sermons on marriage and family—in spite of the pervasive ambivalence, if not outright opposition, to marriage and family in Scripture. Where on earth do preachers like James Dobson find a good biblical text for a sermon entitled "Biblical Principles for a Happy Family"? Most of the families in the Bible are dysfunctional and unhappy. Jesus' disruption of his own family and those of his disciples (to say nothing of Paul's notorious antipathy toward marriage and family) is eschatological. Nothing better illustrates the practical consequences of Jesus' claim that we are living in the time of ending. Commitments that made sense in the old world just don't work the same way in the whole new world. Therefore, time-honored, time-bound practices like marriage and family must be reexamined in the light of "the end." Our recent embrace of the family and marriage in our preaching is testimony to our relaxation of the eschatological tension that once drove the church into more creative thinking about the world and the church.

New Testament Christianity is restlessly, consistently eschatological, and therefore relentlessly political—a claim about who has ultimate power and, by implication, who does not. Our preaching can't be biblical without being a claim about the end of time and a reorienting of present life on the basis of the end. The end will have differing significance for differing groups, depending on where they happen to be when they get news of the end. As Walter Brueggemann notes, for some (the dead and defeated) the eschaton means "new possibility," for others (the powerful and privileged) "a departure," and yet for others (the poor and oppressed) eschaton means "entitlement." For all it will be a stoking, a rearrangement, a fueling of the imagination, reorienting everything now in light of the end.[44]

The key biblical text for a truly Christian assessment of time is 2 Peter 3. To those who scoffed that we are actually living in the "last days" (2 Pet 3:3) the writer notes that their skepticism is based upon their false sense that the cyclic succession of nature is the truth about time. It's been one season after another since the beginning of time; why should nature not continue without interruption (2 Pet 3:4)? The writer counters with remembrance of historical events that were truly decisive, comparing Christ's return to those events (2 Pet 3:5-7). Then the writer vividly depicts the eschatological move from earthly time to eternity (2 Pet 3:7, 10-11). Our time is a paradoxical age in which we are to both wait for and to hasten the "coming of the day of God" (2 Pet 3:12).[45] We must beware of thinking that our sense of time, instilled in us by the chronological passage of natural time, is akin to God's time: "with the Lord one day is like a thousand years, and a thousand years are like one day" (2 Pet 3:8). That's why "the day of the Lord will come like a thief" (2 Pet 3:10).

I agree with Tom Long that "vibrant Christian preaching depends upon the recovery of [an] eschatological voice."[46] Eschatology is not only a claim about the future and who has it, but eschatology is also a claim about agency. The modern world removed God as agent from history. Eschatology says that's a lie. God is yet God. The ingrained liberal resistance to eschatology—based upon liberalism's privileging of the present status quo in modernity over God's promised future—may be our greatest mainline Protestant homiletical challenge.[47] Eschatology keeps things tense, whereas most of us preachers think it our job to relax the tension and the anxiety caused by Jesus. I hope that is why I like to preach sermons that have no neat endings—it keeps things open. I hope that this tendency in my own preaching is due to the nature of the Trinity. Only a living God can move into the future. Only a living God surprises. Only God can properly end a sermon.[48]

I am still haunted by a long conversation I had with a man who was a member of one of my early congregations. He told me that one evening, returning from a night of poker with pals, he had a stunning vision of the presence of the risen Christ. Christ appeared to him undeniably, vividly.

Yet though this event shook him and stirred him deeply, in ten years he had never told anyone about it before he told me, his pastor. I pressed him on his silence. Was he embarrassed? Was he fearful that others would mock him or fail to believe that this had happened to him?

"No," he explained, "the reason why I told no one was I was too afraid that it was true. And if it's true that Jesus was really real, that he had come personally to me, what then? I'd have to change my whole life. I'd have to become some kind of radical or something. And I love my wife and family and was scared I'd have to change, to be somebody else, and destroy my family, if the vision was real."

That conversation reminded me that there are all sorts of reasons for disbelieving the resurrection of crucified Jesus, reasons that have nothing to do with our being modern, scientific, critical people.

The "new" we ought to relish is the eschatological newness that occurs in the repetition of a truth that is so cataclysmic that nobody wants to hear, a truth that the government doesn't want you to know, truth that is so inconvenient that it sets our most elaborate defenses in motion.

What's new? *New* is a people who are willing to keep telling a story that can never be extinguished by being told again because it is a story always out of season, odd, abnormal. The world has a way of restoring the freshness to the story because the story always sounds new to the world. The world lives by a story counter to the ones told in the Bible. The church must never tire of patiently reiterating this story in the face of a world that doesn't get it. No layperson has ever come to church on Christmas or Easter saying, "Preacher, please give me a sermon that's novel, cute, innovative, and breaks new ground."

Perhaps this is because the laity know that a story that claims that Herod got bested by a baby, or that the soldiers were defeated by a crucified Jew are perennially odd. We preachers, who must work with these strange stories so often that they eventually appear to us as normal, must therefore discipline ourselves not to let our pastoral boredom lead us into the temptation to attempt something new in what we say about Good Friday.

"Survey courses are death to professors," an older professor advised me when I began teaching at Duke. "Going over the same material semester after semester will kill you. To stay alive while teaching survey courses you must attempt to listen to the same material as if you are hearing it as a freshman."

No. The challenge is to keep loving the same material so that one is continually refreshed by the material. That's why it is so essential for professors, particularly ones who teach survey courses, to do research and writing so they'll keep being surprised by the same material they must teach. Professors who must deliver the same material, year after year, really do publish or perish.

So Mark begins his Gospel, a story that already had some age on it by the time Mark preached it: "The time is fulfilled, and the kingdom of God has come near; repent, and believe in the good news" (Mark 1:14).

In Jesus "incarnation" was not only in the flesh but also in time. In Jesus Christ God penetrated the time of the Pharisee, the Emperor, the leper, the Scribe, and the prostitute and to all he reiterated the same promise, "Yours is the Kingdom of Heaven." He taught his disciples to begin prayer with a series of eschatological petitions: "Your name now be made holy; your kingdom comes now; and your will done now" (Matt 6:9 paraphrased). He preached the kingdom into the present lives of his hearers, giving them no time for careful consideration or postponement. If you waited too long to respond, at least in Mark's Gospel, Jesus had already moved on somewhere else.

He spoke of the future, but did so by dissolving the temporal distance between future and present. "Follow me," he cried, "and let the dead bury their own dead" (Matt 8:22). He enacted the future at the table, so that you couldn't tell whether the messianic banquet was tomorrow or tonight. He performed miracles for the suffering—enactments, signs, instances of the Kingdom's drawing near, now. He thereby shrank the distance between his mission and the Kingdom. "But if it is by the Spirit of God that I cast out demons, then the kingdom of God has come to you" (Matt 12:28). His preaching was of a *coming* Kingdom but, wherever that preaching was heard, the Kingdom was already. We couldn't keep up with him; still can't, nor are we able to predict where he will show up next, or when he will make himself known in a sermon. We preachers keep preaching in the faith that, despite us, he keeps showing up.[49] Again.

All of which is to say that I'm agreeing with Karl Barth that the newness in the kingdom of God is located in the nature of God: "God . . . will always be new to us. God's kingdom is God . . . as God *comes*."[50]

The church and its preaching are Christ taking our time for himself.

Listen to most Easter hymns and many Easter sermons and you might think that the whole point of Easter is, "Jesus is raised . . . and now we too shall get to go to heaven," with the emphasis decidedly on the second half of that affirmation. This is a strange take on Easter when one considers that the gospel resurrection narratives seem unconcerned about our future hope. Paul drew out a future hope for us as an implication of Jesus' resurrection, but that does not appear to be a first-order interest in Paul and certainly is not an explicit concern of the synoptic Gospels. In a sense, the risen Christ is not so much the one who rescues us now from having one day forever to die but rather he rescues us today from having to live with no hope beyond America.

I've just finished teaching an undergraduate course on Jesus. As part of the course we viewed a number of films on Jesus (including *Jesus of Montreal* and *The Last Temptation of Christ*). The students noted that most of these films have a gritty, first-century, Near Eastern verisimilitude about them—you really believe that you are there. Until they get to the resurrection. At the resurrection the camera becomes unfocused, everything gets fuzzy, blurred, and pastel.

How different from the Gospel narratives of Easter. The Gospels give the story of Easter an utterly this-world, present-age significance. Jesus Christ—whom we crucified—is revealed in his resurrection to be the true Lord of the world, this world, not some future world. Jesus is raised to reign now, not later. Thus the Easter narratives are accounts of vocation. Witnesses of the resurrection have a job to do—to tell the whole world the truth that Jesus Christ is Lord and all other presumed lordlets are not. "Go . . . tell!"

It is as if the Gospel accounts of Easter try not to give encouragement to those who attempt to make Jesus' resurrection an otherworldly, spiritual experience.[51] The Gospels present the resurrection of Jesus as a political event, that which happens here, now in the Gospel mix of fear, misapprehension, evening meals, locked doors, breakfast on the beach, and the disciples' sexist unwillingness to believe the testimony of women. God's new age has broken into the present time, our time. And the first to get the news were not good, spiritually perceptive people; they were people like us. We do not live in a perpetual state of pious Eucharistic adoration; our world is the dreary world of breakfast, soggy cornflakes, doubt, and fear. We gather, in your church and mine, not with spiritually perceptive, fully believing, undoubting Christians; we gather with those who, when it comes to Jesus' resurrection, are convinced that Caesar calls the shots. We are as clueless as Simon Peter, shocked and utterly unprepared that the risen Christ should appear to a loser like him.

This was made manifest for me a few Easters ago. The teenaged son of one of our pastors took his life just before Holy Week. Trying to offer comfort to the pastor and his family during their horrible tragedy, I asked, "Is there anything I can do to help?" The pastor replied, "Would you come to my church and preach the Easter sermon? I'll be in no condition to preach it myself."

My first reaction to his request was a huge sense of ineptitude—is it possible to speak a good word in the face of such horror and grief? Perhaps death really does reign. Upon further reflection it occurred to me that this is always the way it is with Easter preaching. Every Easter we must preach to a world that is always in danger of thinking that death has the last word. Every Easter sermon is preached to people in grief. Every Easter a pastor is forced to speak in behalf of those who are "in no condition to preach it myself." On Easter we preach, throwing our voices up against the tragic, raging against the final enemy one more time. And it is the world's fate to not know the truth about Easter unless some inept preacher like me tells the story. (The women at the tomb, first witnesses to the resurrection, were commanded to "Go . . . tell!" though none of them had sufficient homiletical training for the task. Perhaps sufficient homiletical training is not the key to effective Easter preaching?) In the power of the Holy Spirit, the Easter narratives stand up to death's dominion, defeat, disbelief, the Devil, and time's inexorable march toward oblivion and preach, "He is risen!"

Thus my Easter sermon:

A Sermon: To Galilee

And very early on the first day of the week, when the sun had risen, they went to the tomb. . . . As they entered the tomb, they saw a young man, dressed in a white robe, . . . he said to them, "Do not be alarmed; you are looking for Jesus of Nazareth, who was crucified. He has been raised; . . . he is going ahead of you to Galilee; there you will see him, just as he told you." (Mark 16:2-7)

For I handed on to you as of first importance what I in turn had received: that Christ died for our sins . . . that he was raised on the third day . . . that he appeared to Cephas, then to the twelve. Then he appeared to more than five hundred brothers and sisters at one time. . . . . Then he appeared to James, then to all the apostles. Last of all, . . . he appeared also to me. (1 Cor 15:3-8)

Mark says that on that first Easter, women went to the tomb to pay their last respects to poor, dead Jesus. To their alarm, the body of Jesus was not there. A "young man, dressed in a white robe," told them, "You are looking for Jesus of Nazareth, who was crucified? Well, he isn't here. He is raised. He is going ahead of you to Galilee."

Here's my Easter question for you: *why Galilee?*

Galilee? Galilee is a forlorn, out-of-the-way sort of place. It's where Jesus came from (which in itself was a shock—"Can anything good come out of Galilee?"). Jesus is Galilee's only claim to fame. Jesus spent most of his ministry out in Galilee, the bucolic outback of Judea. He expended most of his teaching trying to prepare his forlorn disciples for their trip up to Jerusalem where the real action was. All of Jesus' disciples seem to have hailed from out in Galilee. Jesus' ultimate goal seems not to focus on Galilee but rather on the capital city, Jerusalem. In Jerusalem he was crucified and in Jerusalem he rose. Pious believers in Jesus' day expected a restoration of Jerusalem in which the Messiah would again make the Holy City the power-center that it deserved to be, the capital city of the world. Which makes it all the more odd that the moment he rose from the dead, says the Gospel scripture, Jesus left the big city and headed back to Galilee. Why?

One might have thought that the first day of his resurrected life the risen Christ might have made straight for the palace, the seat of Roman power, appear there and say, "Pilate, you made a big mistake. Now, it's payback time!"

One might have thought that Jesus would do something effective. If you want to have maximum results, don't waste your time talking to the first person whom you meet on the street, figure out a way to get to the movers and the shakers, the influential and the newsmakers, those who have some power and prestige. If you really want to promote change, go to the top.

I recall an official of the National Council of Churches who, when asked why the Council had fallen on hard times and appeared to have so little influence, replied, "The Bush Administration has refused to welcome us to the White House." How on earth can we get anything done if the most powerful person on earth won't receive us at the White House?

But Jesus? He didn't go up to the palace, the White House, the Kremlin, or Downing Street. He went to Galilee.

Why Galilee? Nobody special lived in Galilee, nobody except the *followers of Jesus. Us.*

The resurrected Christ comes back to and appears before the very same ragtag group of failures who so disappointed him, misunderstood him, forsook him, and fled into the darkness. He returns to his betrayers. He returns to us.

It would have been news enough that Christ had died, but the good news was that he died *for us.* As Paul said elsewhere (Romans 5), one of us might be willing to die for a really good person, but Christ shows that he is not one of us by his willingness to die for sinners like us. His response to our sinful antics was not to punish or judge us. Rather, he came back to us, flooding our flat world not with the wrath that we deserved but with his vivid presence that we did not deserve.

It would have been news enough that Christ rose from the dead, but the good news was that he rose *for us*.

That first Easter, nobody actually saw Jesus rise from the dead. They saw him afterwards. They didn't appear to him; he appeared to them. Us. In the Bible, the "proof" of the resurrection is not the absence of Jesus' body from the tomb; it's the presence of Jesus to his followers. The gospel message of the resurrection is not first, "Though we die, we shall one day return to life," it is, "Though we were dead, Jesus returned to us." If it was difficult to believe that Jesus was raised from the dead, it must have been almost impossible to believe that he was raised and returned *to us*. The result of Easter, the product of the resurrection of Christ is the church—a community of people with nothing more to convene us than that the risen Christ came back to us. That's our only claim, our only hope. He came back to Galilee. He came back to us.

I visit churches where they have a "Seeker Service" on Sunday mornings. Sometimes they have a "Seeker Service" on Saturday night. What's a "Seeker Service"? It's worship trimmed to the limitations of those who don't know much about church, where the music is all singable, and all the ideas are understandable, and the preachers are adorable. It's designed for people who are "seeking" something better in their lives.

Of course the church should reach out to people, including those who seek something better in their lives. Trouble is that's not the way the Bible depicts us. Scripture is not a story about how we kept seeking God. As we demonstrated on Good Friday and Holy Saturday, we can adjust to death. We can get along just fine without Jesus. So back to work, back to what we were doing before Jesus called us, back to Galilee. Nobody expected, even less wanted a resurrection.

But on Easter we were encountered by a Christ who was unwilling to let the story of us and God end in death. Easter is the story about how God keeps—despite us—seeking us.

On Easter, and in the days afterward, the risen Christ showed up among us while we were back at work out in Galilee—when he "appeared to Cephas, then to the twelve. Then he appeared to more than five hundred brothers and sisters at one time, . . . Then he appeared to James, then to all the apostles. Last of all, . . . he appeared also" to the great persecutor and murderer of the church named Paul. The risen Christ was only doing what the crucified Jesus always did: *he came back to us.*

"Show us God!" we demanded of Jesus. God? God is the shepherd who doesn't just sit back and wait for the lost sheep to wander back home, God goes out, seeks, risks everything, beats the bushes night and day, and finds that lost sheep!

God is the father who does not simply fold his hands and sit back and wait for the wayward son to come home; God is the heavenly Father who leaves heaven and reaches down in the mire and pulls out the prodigal son that he may be at home with the Father forever.

We thought, what with the blood and the betrayal of Friday, this was the end. We thought it was over between us and God. At last, we had gone too far away, had stooped to the torturing to death of God's own Son.

Then on Easter, he came back. He came back to the very ones who had forsaken, betrayed, and crucified him. He came back to *us.*

Christians are the people who don't simply know something the world does not yet know, or believe something that nonchristians don't yet believe. We are the people who have had something happen to us that the world appears not yet to have experienced. The risen Christ has come back to us. In one way or another, you are here because the risen Christ sought you, met you, caught you, and commandeered you for God's purposes. We live not alone.

Implications? When we walk through the valley of the shadow of death, time and again we look up and realize that we're not walking by ourselves. When we come to some dead end in life, we look over the brink, into the dark abyss, and, to our surprise and delight, there he is, awaiting us, a light in the darkness. We pick up the morning newspaper and delude ourselves that if we can just get some really good political leadership, some really effective defensive weapons all our problems will be solved. Then comes the risen Christ who confronts and overpowers those politicos who thought they were in charge. We give up, give in, despair only to be surprised to find him near to us.

A student, asked to summarize the gospel in a few words, responded: in the Bible, it gets dark, then it gets very, very dark, then Jesus shows up. I'd add to this affirmation, Jesus doesn't just show up; he shows up *for us.*

As the psalmist declared:

Where can I go from your spirit?
  Or where can I flee from your presence?
If ascend to heaven, you are there;
  If I make my bed in Sheol, you are there. (Ps 139:7-8)

I was visiting a man as he lay dying, his death only a couple of days away. I asked him there at the end what he was feeling. Was he fearful?

"Fear? No," he responded, "I'm not fearful because of my faith in Jesus."

"We all have hope that our future is in God's hands," I said, somewhat piously.

"Well, I'm not hopeful because of what I believe about the future," he corrected me, "I'm hopeful because of what I've experienced in the past."

I asked him to say more.

"I look back over my life, all the mistakes I've made, all the times I've turned away from Jesus, gone my own way, strayed, and got lost. And time and again, he found a way to get to me, showed up and got me, looked for me when I wasn't looking for him. I don't think he'll let something like my dying defeat his love for me."

There was a man who understood Easter.

To the poor, struggling Corinthians, failing at being the church, back-sliding, wandering, split apart, faithless, scandalously immoral, Paul preaches Easter. He reminds them that they are here, *ekklesia*, gathered and summoned by the return of the risen Christ. Earlier, God declared, "I will be their God and they will be my people." That's the story that, by the sheer grace of God, continues. That's what this risen Savior does. He comes back—again and again—to the very ones (I'm talking about us!) who so betray and disappoint him. He appears to us, seeks us, finds, grabs us, embraces, holds on to us, commissions us to do his work. In returning to his disciples, the risen Christ makes each of us agents of Easter. "As the Father has sent me," Jesus says, "so I send you" (John 20:21).

What the young man in white tells the women is in effect, "Jesus is raised! You had better get yourselves back to Galilee, there you will see him." This was a wonderful, frightening thing to hear: the risen Christ is at work, on the loose, and will appear where you live. By the way, Christians, from the first, seem to have worshiped on Sunday. Sunday for Jews was not a holy day of rest; it was the first day of the Jewish work-week. Isn't it curious that Jesus wasn't raised on a Saturday, a holy day, but was raised on the day when everybody went back to work? I think in so doing God demonstrated that faithfulness is the willingness to be con-fronted by Christ even at the office. Jesus is raised into our time and our place. Now every day is sanctified and the whole creation, even Alabama, is the holy land. From this perspective, tomorrow, Easter Monday may be more to the point than Easter itself.

In life, in death, in any life beyond death, this is our great hope and our great commission. Hallelujah! Go! Tell! The risen Christ came back to Birmingham—uh, I mean, *Galilee*.

CHAPTER THREE

REPETITION

Therefore every scribe, who has been trained for the
kingdom of heaven is like the master of a household
who brings out of his treasure what is new and
what is old.[1] *(Matthew 13:52)*

When Paul preached at Antioch, people pled, "Please preach that sermon again next week" (Acts 13:42). What a curious request. Nobody ever said to me, "Great sermon! Let's do it one more time on Monday, same time, same place, same sermon."

It's even more curious when one considers Paul's sermon in Acts 13—an uncreative rehash of Paul's previous Acts sermons. Moreover, who was the audience for this sermon? Surely it was the church. In other words, the audience already knew the content of the sermon, had already heard it all before.

And yet, they asked Paul to say it again. Perhaps the church knew, even in its infancy, that faithful preaching is always repetitious reiteration, always preaching *again*.

A sermon is more like a workday breakfast than a fancy state dinner. Preaching ought to stick with us for the long term. A sermon is cumulative nourishment. Most of us shun innovation at breakfast. Nobody says, "Cornflakes with milk? *Again*?" Breakfast is not intended to be original or life changing. (Show me somebody who expects excitement at breakfast and I'll show you someone who . . . well . . .) Preaching is meant to be nourishment for the long haul, life sustaining. The story that preaching tells is renewing, but not new. Jesus said he was the "bread of life," not the flaming cherries jubilee of life. Ordinary bread sustains. One of the few things that Jesus gave us permission to pray for on a daily basis, by rote, repetitiously, without thinking about it, was bread.

That's why a chief homiletical virtue is persistence—faithfulness over time. Preaching is not to be judged for its immediate impact but for its cumulative effect.[2] I've been the recipient of my wife's culinary arts for what, six thousand meals? The meals I most remember are not that multifaceted meal we had one Thanksgiving or the French feast she pulled off one Saturday night. It is the daily, constant acts of love that are all the meals that she created over time. Families are held together by mealtimes, not because they are special or spectacular, but because they are so wonderfully ordinary, normal, and typical. In my experience, people with a terminal illness rarely want to see Paris or jet to Tahiti; what they most desire is a dozen more weekday breakfasts with the family.

This is similar to my response to those Methodists who whine, "But if we have the Lord's Supper every Sunday, won't it seem less special?"

The Lord's Supper is the normal food of Christians. It's not supposed to feel special. It is supposed to be the most natural thing in the world, your destiny. We therefore take care to pray the same Eucharistic prayer over and over again with the same words. This is the core story, that which convenes us. So we want to be sure that we get it right and leave out nothing of import. Besides, the Eucharist is not predicated on what you feel about Jesus but rather on how Jesus feels about you. We pray this prayer not primarily to stir up in us religious sentiment but rather to name who God is by recitation of what God does.

One of my favorite Russian authors is Leo Tolstoy. Tolstoy is known for his deliberate, frequent, and sometimes exasperating repetitiveness. Literary critic R. F. Christian notes that Tolstoy repeats the same word no less than five times in a sentence in dozens of different sentences. Tolstoy also repeats a particular mannerism of a character every time he returns to that character. Sometimes Tolstoy appears to be repetitive in the interest of rhythm. For instance, in the death of Prince Andrei, Tolstoy uses the words "weep" or "wept" almost a dozen times in just a few paragraphs, almost like a refrain in a song. The repetition fixes the character in our minds while telling such a large, long, and unwieldy story as *War and Peace*. A more significant reason for Tolstoy's repetition is that Tolstoy seems to be searching, probing his characters, returning to them again, redescribing them, adding to our knowledge of them with each recurring encounter. His repetition has the effect of creating another world for us in which to dwell where the literature gives us the luxury of going back to the same mysterious characters over and over in an obstinate attempt to understand.

A major function of Israel's Scripture is the transmission of the tradition, the exercise of memory through creative repetition and reiteration. Of the statutes of Israel it is said, "We will not hide them from their children; / we will tell to the coming generation / the glorious deeds of the LORD, and his might . . . / that the next generation might know them, the children yet unborn . . . / that they should not be like their ancestors, / a stubborn and rebellious generation" (Ps 78:4-8). The tradition is reiterated, not simply in the interest of repeating the past but so that we might change the present and not be like our grandparents, "a stubborn and rebellious generation."

> Keep these words that I am commanding you today in your heart. Recite them to your children and talk about them when you are at home and when you are away, when you lie down and when you rise. Bind them as a sign on your hand, fix them as an emblem on your forehead, and write them on the doorposts of your house and on your gates. (Deut 6:6-9)

Walter Brueggemann marvels that in Israel, the urgency of transmitting the glories of the tradition is matched by supple and imaginative creativity in that transmission. The tradition was not merely handed on but reformulated in order that what was past might be vividly present. Somehow Israel managed to avoid "frozen, flattened fundamentalism" as well as "dismissive indifference" in regard to its treasured past. Israel managed to remember with wonderment.[3]

Early Christian preachers not only continued this Hebrew wonderment with ancient texts but added to it the astounding claim that, after Jesus, Christians understood Israel's ancient texts even better than Israel, or at least in a radically invigorated way. On a regular basis the church gathers and hears texts that were generated over two thousand years ago, reading them as if they pertain specifically and authoritatively to us today. Richard Hays, in his masterful study of Paul's use of Scripture, says, "The text was written by some human author long ago, written to and for an ancient community of people in Israel but original writer and readers have become types whose meaning emerges with full clarity only in the church—that is, only in the empirical eschatological community that Paul is engaging in building. Even utterances that appear to be spoken to others in another time find their true addressees in us."[4]

"Do I contradict myself?" asks Walt Whitman in *Leaves of Grass*. "Very well then I contradict myself."[5] We preachers must have the confidence to do the same.[6]

I know a young man who saw *The Matrix* thirty times. I saw *The Matrix* once, found it "clever," that is, "new" and therefore felt no need to see it again. When all you've got is "new," once is enough. However, this young man found *The Matrix* to be revealing, deep, and disrupting and therefore delighted in seeing it again and again. He thrilled in seeing the same thing but this time seeing something that he had missed before. Sometimes he simply delighted in seeing the same secret he had discovered in a previous viewing but this time seeing the secret again as an insider who has been let in on the enigma. The repetition that made repeating *The Matrix* pointless to me was part of its power for him, the power of repetition rather than of dullness. Once is never enough for truth that is cataclysmic.

At the beginning of his *Tractatus Logicus* Wittgenstein said that he was only attempting to think what people had already thought. He claimed that his philosophical tract "will be understood only by someone who has already had these thoughts or at least thoughts similar to these thoughts."[7] The peculiar power of Wittgenstein's philosophical insights is in their being so brilliantly commonplace and obvious, except that we never thought about these matters in this way until we thought about them with him. He felt that what passed for philosophy had put cataracts in our eyes so that we stood before a tree, questioning if it were really a tree when what we should have been doing is looking at the tree! In that sense, to encounter a tree is always to reencounter the tree.

Perhaps no one can communicate, in any depth, something that is not already known, at some depth. Plato said that all teaching is a form of midwifery. We can't really think that which has not somehow already resided in us. All thought is therefore a sort of repetition, according to Plato. All thought is thought from the inside out.[8]

I see Plato's point. We tend to move forward in our thought by way of digression. If I think in words that are English, in images and feelings that are derivative of past experience whereby I learned to use the English language, then all human thought is, to a great degree midwifery, exercise in repetition. We speak and think out of habit.[9] Only that thought that is revelation is new thought, thought from outside of our experience. In most of our thinking, thoughts repeat themselves. This is our accustomed way of understanding—through Tolstoy-like repetition in which we circle around ideas and re-circle, circling again and again.

Sometime in 1880 Rodin returned from a trip to Italy and began work on a massive set of doors for a planned museum in Paris. Though the doors were never finished, a few of the figures he sculpted for the doors survive, including his massive, "Adam." Rodin's "Adam" is a direct quote from Michelangelo's fresco of the creation of Adam on the ceiling of the Sistine Chapel—Adam's massive hands, his languid pose, his body just beginning to move with life. Yet Michelangelo's Adam is itself a quote from Jacopo della Quercia's small "Creation of Adam" bronze panel. This is often the way of great art. Rarely is an artistic creation completely new; each work of art is beholden to another's work. Most fine works of art involve creative quotation.

I was therefore surprised to read Norman Mailer's notion that little good comes of repetition:

> [R]epetition kills the soul. . . . Any number of kinds of repetition are, I will admit, crucial to the human venture. It is, after all, one of the ways by which we learn. And there is such a thing as creative repetition. Nonetheless, I'm suspicious of ritual. Where, after all, does my theology start? What occasions it? What stimulates it? I would answer that it is because I've worked as a novelist all my life. . . . Now, where in all this is the relation to ritual? Ritual is repetition, and in writing a novel you look to do the opposite. A fine novel does not keep repeating itself. That is exactly the hallmark of a dull work. So most good novelists are wary of repetition. Moreover, most people I don't approve of tend to be masters or monsters of mediocre repetition. The politicians we despise are one example. So one develops an understanding that repetition can be dangerous when used as a tool for mediocre purposes. Unimaginative parents often know nothing better than to repeat what they say over and over.[10]

Mailer's derision of repetition as soul-killing is odd since so many of his best works involve titles, plots, themes, and characters that are purloined. Perhaps his gargantuan vanity led Mailer to think that what he thought was thought up on his own.

Film theorist Bruce Kawin distinguishes between "repetitious" and "repetitive." "Repetitious," says Kawin, occurs "when a word, percept, or experience is repeated with less impact at each recurrence; repeated to no particular end, out of a lack of intention or sloppiness of thought."

On the other hand, "repetitive happens when a word, precept or experience is repeated with equal or greater force at each occurrence."[11] The repetitive is characterized by intention, self-awareness. Repetition counts on the listener to recognize the repetitiveness and to rejoice in that recognition. Repetition seeks to revitalize the elements of the originating source so that they can be seen anew. Therefore, creativity and repetition go hand in hand. It is the joy of hearing the same story retold, and realizing that the retelling is not only enlarging the story as first heard but is also remaking the story. The repetitiveness draws us in and engages us as we look for fresh interpretations of the same story. The informed listener experiences a certain degree of pleasure in being able to recognize the allusions and the inside jokes.

I figure that most of Scripture was addressed to the informed listener, the gathered congregation, those who were already practitioners of the faith. It is rare that Scripture has much apologetic interest in speaking to the uninitiated. Ernst Haenchen theorized that the Acts of the Apostles was an early "apologia to the Roman Empire," reassuring Romans that they had nothing to fear from these Christians. I find this theory of Acts' intent to be bizarre. It's hard to imagine a Roman bureaucrat like Felix or Agrippa plowing through Acts out of curiosity about Christians. No, Acts is, foremost, testimony by the informed to the initiated that they may grow in their understanding and inculcation of the faith.

Apologetics tends to eschew repetition of the themes and stories of Scripture but fails to get beyond basing its arguments on the repetition of non-scriptural (pagan) arguments. I suspect that contemporary homiletics' attempt (PowerPoint Preaching) to practice apologetics and make sermons completely comprehensible to the uninitiated is responsible for the theological vacuity of much contemporary preaching. It's hard to get the uninitiated initiated on the basis of extrabiblical reasoning that is fundamentally at odds with the gospel. I actually heard a preacher say that he intentionally constructed his sermons so that they could be interesting and readily understood by any sixteen year old. Knowing this pastor, I'm certain that he succeeded in fulfilling his intentions.

G. K. Chesterton once said that Almighty God is a bit like a young child, saying every single morning to the sun, "Again!" Like a little child, God delights in repetition, never tires of having the world repeat Genesis 1 and creation. Each morning, with infant-like glee, God says to the world, "Do it again!"

Every discovery is a recovery. Discovery consists in the interface, within the mind, of certain old pieces of information that have been received from the past. Repeated old ideas, when they interface with one another, sometimes conflict, produce sparks, and thereby fabricate new ideas. Therefore, a major assignment for Christian preaching is constant engagement with the past, particularly past texts. In each retelling, the past is being remixed, remade, re-presented.[12] Paul asks repeatedly "Do you not know?" (1 Cor 5:6, 6:2, etc.). Paul implies that the Corinthians ought to know. So he reminds them in order really to know. Most preaching, even preaching as early as Paul's, is reiteration.

The Rhetoric of Repetition

Good preachers utilize repetition as a rhetorical strategy for producing emphasis, clarity, amplification, or emotional effect in sermons.[13] The art of rhetoric is replete with terms that point to specific sorts of repetitive speech acts (*conduplicatio*).[14]

1. We repeat sounds and letters (Evangelicals from Fuller Seminary were once masters of this):

alliteration	Repetition of the same sound at the beginning of two or more stressed syllables.
assonance	Repetition of similar vowel sounds, preceded and followed by different consonants, in the stressed syllables of adjacent words.
homoioteleuton	Similarity of endings of adjacent or parallel words.
paroemion	Alliteration taken to an extreme—every word in a sentence begins with the same consonant.
paromoiosis	Parallelism of sound between the words of adjacent clauses whose lengths are equal or approximate to one another.

2. We repeat words (Abraham Lincoln and Martin Luther King[15] were masters at this, as is the Old Testament):

anadiplosis	The repetition of the last word of one clause or sentence at the beginning of the next.
anaphora	Repetition of the same word or group of words at the beginning of successive clauses, sentences, or lines.
antanaclasis	The repetition of a word whose meaning changes in the second instance.

conduplicatio	The repetition of a word or words in adjacent phrases or clauses, either to amplify the thought or to express emotion.
diacope	Repetition of a word with one or more between, usually to express deep feeling.
epanalepsis	Repetition at the end of a line, phrase, or clause of the word or words that occurred at the beginning of the same line, phrase, or clause.
epistrophe	Ending a series of lines, phrases, clauses, or sentences with the same word or words. The opposite of anaphora.
epizeuxis	Repetition of words with no others between.
mesarchia	The repetition of the same word or words at the beginning and middle of successive sentences.
polysyndeton	Employing many conjunctions between clauses.

3. And we repeat ideas (St. Paul is a master of this):

commoratio	Dwelling on or returning to one's strongest argument.
disjunctio	A similar idea is expressed with different verbs in successive clauses.
epanodos	Repeating the main terms of an argument in the course of presenting it.
epimone	Persistent repetition of the same plea in much the same words.
expolitio	Repetition of the same idea, changing either its words, its delivery, or the general treatment it is given.
scesis onomaton	A series of successive, synonymous expressions.

I'll admit that, in our rhetoric of repetition, we preachers are often guilty of *tautologia* (repetition of the same idea in different words in a wearisome or unnecessary way), and *homiologia* (tedious, inane, unvarying repetition), and even *pleonasmus* (using more words than is necessary). Of all these, I am a master.

Knowledge as Repetition

And yet, repetition may be more than a preacher trick, a savvy rhetorical strategy. Repetition may be a deep way of knowing. Søren Kierkegaard wrote a curious work on this subject: *Repetition: A Venture in Experimenting Psychology* (1843).[16] The treatise is written in the voice of Constantin Constantius. In *Either/Or*[17] Kierkegaard had said, "There is no such thing as repetition. The only thing repeated was the impossibility of repetition."[18] Time consumes everything. The idea of "now" is mostly a human construct to defend ourselves against the ravages of time. The present is past in an instant and what is past cannot really be made to live again. There can be no recovery.

In *Repetition* Kierkegaard engages in a more careful look at the nature of repetitiveness. I assume that S.K.'s purpose was to nuance the platonic concept of thinking as remembrance, the linkage of knowledge with memory, and the platonic notion that insight is retrogressive recollection. As we have noted, Plato taught that all our knowledge consists of remembrance of the eternal ideals implanted in the soul. The ideals are innate and await evocation in the mind. Education (Latin: *educare*) is midwifery that delivers these ideals. For Plato, when we think we have had a fresh insight, in truth we have simply remembered what we already knew.

Perhaps S.K. was contrasting platonic knowledge-as-recollection with faith as it meets us in Jesus Christ. For S.K. repetition is not some nostalgic attempt to retrieve the past; it is a means by which we become different people. Kierkegaard said that "genuine repetition is recollected forward." I project myself into the future through recollection of the past. "Modern philosophy will teach that all life is a repetition."[19] By repeating some notion, I am taking it back from the past, thrusting this idea into the future. Repetition and recollection are two different directions of the very same movement: both repetition and memory involve the same action, one toward our future and the other our past.

Kierkegaard uses the figures of Job and Abraham as parables that help in understanding peculiarly Jewish/Christian repetition. Deep knowledge involves privation, acceptance, and repair. The first step toward knowing is not knowing; it is awareness of ignorance and emptiness, *privation*. The path to having is through the recognition that we are bereft. Job regains everything that was stripped from him only after his great moment of resignation that he had lost everything. Abraham gets Isaac back in the instant that he lets Isaac go. It is in the process of loss (*privation*), recognition of loss (*acceptance*), and wondrous restoration (*repair*) that the individual's sense of that which is lost and regained becomes intense and authentic. Only through loss of self can we have our true selves. Abraham got his son back, but not at all in the same way that his son once was to him. Job got God back, but not really the same God, certainly not in the same relationship, as before. *Privation, acceptance,* and *repair.* This is repetition in the sense that the Renaissance was rejuvenation of classical Greece and Rome. The culture that was thoroughly lost was regained, repeated in a vivid, essential way, but only after it was acknowledged as lost.

Rising above the superficiality of the aesthete and the dreariness of the ethical, repetition, as S.K. thinks of it, is an aspect of the religious stage. Repetition is a "religious mood" that raises our way of thinking and being exponentially. Repetition is part of our will to become. It is a way of claiming the present as significant by reclaiming the past as present. We go backwards just enough truly to move forward.

We cannot know Abraham; he is lost to us. Yet, in reclaiming Abraham, through our preaching about Abraham, we regain not only Abraham but also ourselves remade. True repetition, true regaining of the past as a present that changes our future, is a gift. We cannot have the past, in this vivifying way, through historical retrieval. It comes to us only as gift. Repetition enables recognition of our selves as those who are always dying, always losing the present to the past, but without anxiety— with faith and love. What we regain is a meaning-saturated world whose power and potential exceed what could be there in the mere present. We receive an unexpected, wondrous restoration in the face of a perceived loss and this restoration brings about a considerably heightened self-consciousness. Abraham's son was restored to him in his relinquishment of him, but restored to him in a very different way. There was a deep sense in which Abraham was no longer the same person, no longer living in the same world once he relinquished his beloved son, then received his son back. So in repetition not only the past is regained but the present as well.

Repetition is thus about becoming. Normally, says S.K., we think of imitation as the path to becoming. I imitate those whom one day I hope to be. But repetition is more dynamic than imitation. Repetition brings to light our predicament. Instead of bemoaning our own belatedness in knowing Jesus, wishing for some return to a sentimentally imagined religious past that is forever lost, in repetition we embrace the present and life in the present, and in so doing we discover Jesus beside us into the future. The God whom we thought was lost to us in the past is now present to us as gift, but only through privation, acceptance of that privation, and repair. To repeat: for S.K. repetition is not simply a heuristic device (something helpful for learning) but is a methodological dictum that has material consequences. He is making a theological claim here.

In a wonderful sermon on the parable of the Pharisee and the tax collector (Luke 18:9-14) Kierkegaard highlights, not the humility of the tax collector, but rather his distance from God, indeed his distance from his fellow humanity.[20] The penitent tax collector is a man who has lost God and knows his loss. It is only after his breast-beating sense of lostness that the man is "justified," brought close to God. The sinful tax collector is made right with God through privation, acceptance of privation, and repair.

This sort of recollection enables us to begin anew, to reclaim ourselves as new selves. Though Kierkegaard doesn't, I might note that preachers thus read us into the biblical story. We are not reading ourselves back into some golden age, going backwards, but we are rather claiming our age as the time of God's presence. Any "golden age" of faith is now moving forward.

S.K. said slyly that *Repetition*, if he had written it as he had hoped, would prove to be a quickly written, witty, plainspoken book that would be possibly incomprehensible to heretics. The motto of *Repetition* is "On wild trees the flowers are odorous, on tame ones the fruit." Constantin Constantius—a modern, objective, analytical psychologist—takes up the "case" of a love-struck young man who, though obsessed with a young woman, cannot bring himself finally to consummate his love for his beloved by marrying her. He fears that if he married her, his love—which now is all yearning, sighing, longing, and potential—would be realized and would soon become boring. He feels more love for her in remembering her in absence than in having her presence in the flesh. Mundane, dutiful marriage might destroy his sense of romance. Marriage would force him to give himself only to one person, that is, he would be forced to repeat himself and in that boring connubial sameness, his love would wilt. He would rather be a poet, experiencing love in the abstract, than a husband, experiencing love as a quotidian commitment in time. Better, he thinks, to love without continuity or being caught in the humdrum repetitiveness of married life, to love her in recollection, to keep love a matter of momentary, fleeting feeling rather than to confine himself to the dulling duty of marriage. The only thing to do, therefore, is to abandon his love, not to be with her but only to recollect her, to keep her a poetic memory, relishing that moment. This must be the "heresy" that S.K. wants to assail in *Repetition*.

Kierkegaard implies that while the distance of recollection is sweet, true love must dare to expose itself to repetition, must attempt to survive over time if it is truly love. Thus the opening motto—wild trees have a spontaneous sweetness about their flowers; but cultivated trees produce the good fruit. Truth is that which can withstand repetition without degenerating into boredom. Truth is that thought that has the capacity continually to rise up, to refuse to be relegated to the past, but also to endure the test of time so that it is able to be fruitful, to speak, to vivify, and to not bore us to death.

In *Repetition* S.K. also contrasts the delusions of "hope"—"a new garment, starched and stiff and glittering, but it has never yet been worn," a garment that may or may not look well on our frame or even fit us at all— and the contrasting delusion of "memory"—"an old garment, and quite useless, however beautiful; for it has been outgrown." *Repetition* "is an imperishable garment, fitting intimately." *Hope* is a beautiful woman who "slips through your fingers" and *memory* is "a handsome old dowager, never quite serving the purpose of the moment." In contrast to ethereal hope or pointless memory, *repetition* is "a beloved wife, of whom one never tires." Wild trees smell sweet but trees cultivated over time produce the fruit.

Yet there is even more to *Repetition*. After the end of the affair, when the poetic young lover picks up a newspaper and learns that his beloved has married another, he feels an odd sense of wholeness. There is loss, but also recovery. He claims his self for himself. And although he doubts anyone else would desire to be him or be in hs present condition and might even see him as discarded, he sees his soul coming back to its proper place, no longer divided, and experiences what he calls a "unified personality." The repetition in this scene is a rebirth, a returning of wholeness to his soul. Privation, acceptance, and repair.

"I risk my life, each moment lose it, and again win it," says the young man who now, having lost his beloved, has her again, but in a very different way. More important, he has a different self as well. *Privation, acceptance,* and *repair.* As you know, Kierkegaard depicted life as stages—the *aesthetic*, the *ethical*, and the *religious*. Repetition makes boredom a danger both for the ethical stage and the aesthetic stage. The aesthete tries to solve the boredom problem with gimmicks in a vain attempt to give some spice to life in order to ward off boredom. The aesthete thus flits from one sweet-smelling—but alas, quickly fading—flower to the next, never alighting anywhere, unable to preserve a feeling over time. For his part, the ethicist becomes a bore through his extreme delight in consistency and pattern. By doing his duty and obeying the rules, the ethicist attempts to give order to life, to tidy up time. Morbid boredom is the result.

Let us preachers take note that S.K. said "only the new" tires. Only the novel gets old. Only "when the mind is engrossed with the old it achieves happiness. He only finds a genuine happiness who refuses to delude himself into thinking that repetition ought to yield him something new; of this illusion boredom is the inevitable consequence."

"Whoever fails to understand that life is repetition, and that this is its beauty," is "lost," says S.K. He posits that we need our repetition as much as we need food and shelter. In a real sense, repetition should be counted among our daily necessities, and we cannot be content or happy without it.

> Who could wish to be subject to everything that is new and flighty, or wish forever to be the vehicle for an ephemeral pleasure? If God had not willed repetition the world would never have come into being. . . . In repetition inheres the earnestness and reality of life. Whoever wills repetition proves himself to be in possession of a pathos that is serious and mature.[21]

This helps explain why the practice of the Christian faith is inherently and exuberantly repetitious. Christians are those who believe that Jesus Christ is not only the way and the life but also the truth who rises from the dead and keeps coming back to us, not precisely as he came to those before us, for his resurrected self is more than a pious memory. He makes himself present to us, now. In resurrection, Christ repeats himself.

"We Can Only Repeat Ourselves"

Thus Karl Barth began his mammoth *Church Dogmatics* with an unashamed promise to be repetitive: "We can only repeat ourselves."[22]

Stanley Hauerwas, in his Gifford Lectures, comments that Barth's statement is "but an indication of his discovery that the God who has found us in Jesus Christ is the subject of Christian theology."[23] God is the true subject of theology — the speaking, vivifying subject who refuses to be silenced. Barth circles his subject (God in Jesus Christ) again and again, in ever widening re-description.[24] All faithful theology can be truthful re-description because God is a living, constantly revealing subject. All faithful theology must be re-description because the only thing that needs to be said about God is that which only God can speak, has spoken, and will speak.

That which happens in Jesus Christ is God "entire and perfect";[25] Christ's saving death "cannot and need not be continued or repeated or added to or superseded."[26] Christ is a "unique history" that manages to be both "new and eternal."[27] Christ is therefore never a "process,"[28] something that grows through gradual degrees and accretions. Nor does Christ need to be re-presented by some means outside himself, for Christ is not lacking in anything nor is he awaiting some further attestation.[29] Repetition, rather than progress or development, is the guiding metaphor for faith in Christ. Therefore, when we preachers speak of Christ, we can only repeat God's perfect, completed, final work—Christ.

The idea of theology as repetition accounted for Barth's definition of the preacher as herald—the preacher is the mere mouthpiece for the proclamation of the King. The preacher is conduit for the message from God to the hearers.[30] As Tom Long notes, "Herald preachers, . . . do not strive to create more beautiful and more excellent sermons; they seek to be more faithful to the message they receive in scripture."[31]

Barth loved the music of Mozart for its circularity, the way Mozart picks up a theme, repeats the theme, adds something to it, leaves it for a time, returns to it, widens it, reiterates and explores its many dimensions. One of the functions of repetition in Barth's theology is to slow us down in order to help us be more attentive. That is hard for us. Modern people lack hope and "don't take long looks at anything," said Flannery O'Connor.[32]

Proust does repetition so well in his writing, and so does Jane Austin. Maybe all great writers do. It is as if they put a microscope on things, magnifying something that is very small, something liable not to be noticed, in order to illuminate the whole, in order to be more panoramic. "My soul magnifies the Lord," sings Mary in her Magnificat. That's what faithful theology does—takes time to attend to God and thereby magnifies God.

But we must take care to note that for Barth, repetition was more than a rhetorical stratagem—it was a theological affirmation. Barth charged that by attempting to avoid the possibility of boring repetition, we preachers are in danger of sidestepping the peculiar "God who has found us in Jesus Christ." Barth says that in our preaching of Christ:

> We can only describe Him again, and often, and in the last resort infinitely often. . . . We can only speak of it again and again in different variations as God in His true revelation gives us part in the truth of His knowing, and therefore gives our knowing similarity with His own, and therefore truth. . . . we have no last word to speak. . . . Jesus Christ is really too good to let Himself be introduced and used as the last word of our self-substantiation.[33]

Barth suggests that there is a word for my desire to be fresh, new, and interesting in the pulpit. The word is *idolatry*. My homiletical attempts to substantiate God in a way that grips my audience is also another attempt at utilizing Jesus Christ in a vain effort at "self-substantiation." My preacherly self (or the selves within my congregation) becomes more important in the process of gospel communication than Christ, the Agent of proclamation.[34] I attempt, through my rhetoric, to force the gospel to speak to those to whom it may have no intention of speaking. How typical of modernity to validate the message on the basis of the speaker's intention or the hearer's reaction, to be more interested in the effect upon the viewer than in what is viewed. Besides, all Christianity comes to us through tradition, because of the loving repetition of this true story by the saints. Since Easter, the truth that is Jesus Christ requires witnesses, someone to pass it on, someone courageous enough to repeat the story. None of us can have Jesus on our own terms. As Barth continually stressed, we must receive Jesus as he is offered to us by the tradition, as he is in himself, not as we would adapt him to be for us. "We can only describe Him again, and often, and in the last resort infinitely often." Therefore we preachers must discipline ourselves to repeat ourselves.

True, our repetition is speaking the gospel "again and again in different variations." N. T. Wright construes biblical authority as similar to that of a play that has five acts but for some reason the fifth act has been lost.[35] A group of actors attempt to perform the play as a whole, adding a fifth act on the basis of what they have learned from the first four acts. The "authority" of the first four acts of the play wouldn't consist of a command that the actors simply repeat, over and over again, the earlier acts.

Rather the drama would contain its own inner consistency and forward movement, to which the actors, in devising the last act, would be faithful. They would need to act with "both innovation and consistency." Christians are those who are living into the last act of the drama that is Scripture. To be faithful to the text, there must be consistency with the intention and the direction of the text, yet there must also be some degree of innovation because the God we are repeating is a living God. Scripture doesn't want simply to be repeated but rather to be embodied, enacted, performed in the light of Easter.

I do wonder if we preachers engage in homiletical calisthenics in our sermons, devising all sorts of intellectual props for the gospel, because we are attempting to enable the gospel to make sense apart from the living, breathing, embodied Christian community that makes Scripture make sense. In other words, are we guilty of deluding ourselves into thinking that we must work hard to keep our preaching fresh and interesting when the main thing Scripture wants to do is to be edifying to the saints who are busy being scriptural people? Perhaps our greatest need in our biblical interpretation is not a better sense of eschatology but a more active engagement in mission? The goal of preaching is embodiment, discipleship more than mere intellectual assent or aesthetic appreciation.

I recently watched a violinist play Vivaldi. She was utterly absorbed by the music on the printed page, her whole body in motion from what she saw with her eyes, vision being transferred through the brain to her fingers, all conveyed to the instrument she played. While she was completely attentive, ardently faithful to each note on the page, she also gave the music an interpretation that was her own—she seemed to play the piece with particular energy and heightened tempo.

I thought this violinist was a good parable of us preachers. We preach while being thoroughly attentive to the biblical text, honoring the details, bowing to the specifics, playing the notes as they are printed, so to speak. But we also give the text our interpretation, both in what we say and how we say it. We want to be original, faithful to our own gifts and insights, but we want to be even more faithful to the text as we have received it. Our preaching is "repetition" in a manner similar to the way that violinist repeated Vivaldi.

In repeating God in sermons we are following a peculiarly biblical way of presenting the truth. Scripture delights in re-presentation and reverberation. John 1 echoes and reflects, expands and reiterates Genesis 1. Creation begins with the pushing back of the dark, chaotic waters of the sea; Revelation ends with the complete defeat of chaos in which "the sea [shall be] no more" (Rev 21:1). There are twelve tribes in Israel; Jesus calls twelve disciples. Moses comes down a mountain with the Ten Commandments; Jesus goes up a mountain to deliver the Beatitudes. Elijah gives bread to a poor widow (1 Kgs 17); Jesus gives bread to the poor multitudes. Manna is given to Israel in the wilderness; Jesus leads the multitudes into the wilderness where he gives bread (Mark 6:30-44) and urges us to pray for "daily bread" like manna. "Christ our passover is sacrificed for us," says Paul. "Therefore let us keep the feast" (1 Cor 5:7-8 KJV), and everyone understood the Lord's Supper in a new way and no one in his congregation ever looked at the Passover in quite the same way ever again.

We can say the gospel again because, in his resurrection, Jesus Christ literally repeats himself. He defeats time, rises up, returns in fresh form, and addresses us, speaks as if he is redoing the gospel.[36] We can speak, as preachers, because Jesus Christ speaks himself anew whenever we dare to repeat the gospel. Every report of the gospel is a repeat of the gospel is resurrection of the gospel by Christ. By the sending of the Spirit, Jesus Christ makes us into "contemporaries" of his finished, perfected history so that we actually live in him here and now.[37] Even the eyewitnesses who came to the tomb on Easter morning did not understand the resurrection. They required the gift of faith in order to be truly contemporary with Jesus. The Holy Spirit is that which enables contemporaeity. Barth defines "eschatological" as "looking into the furthest and final future, and from there back again into the present."[38]

Thus Easter is the basis of preaching, the only hope for preaching's possibility. We can preach, our people can hear because of the agent of preaching, that is, the risen Christ. Jesus said to us humble preachers: "It is not you who speak, but the Spirit of your Father speaking through you" (Matt 10:20). "Whoever listens to you listens to me, and whoever rejects you rejects me" (Luke 10:16). That's claiming a great deal for us preachers! We can and must repeat ourselves in the pulpit. We preachers can be so bold because of faith that there is only one preacher, Christ. And he will preach.

That's why Barth said that the best we preachers can do is to just attempt to preach, try to preach, for none of us can really preach Christ.[39] It is only proclamation when the Holy Spirit descends and takes up the work of preaching. Only Christ can preach Christ. And he will preach.

The poet laments the difficulty of bringing difficult truth to speech:

> So here I am, . . . having had twenty years . . .
> Trying to learn to use words, and every attempt
> Is a wholly new start, and a different kind of failure . . .
> Is a new beginning, a raid on the inarticulate
> With shabby equipment always deteriorating. . . . [40]

As preacher here I am, having wasted not twenty years (like T. S. Eliot) but nearly twice that many "trying to use words." And every attempt to say again what the saints have said before is, in its own way, a "wholly new start," as well as another failure, but failure of a different kind. We preachers keep launching weekly "raids on the articulate." We stutter and stammer, mutter and jammer because we are trying to talk about God with such shabby, faltering equipment.

Such is our fate. And yet, by God's grace, our fate is transformed into our vocation. Christ incarnates in human speech. Christ is raised into human time. We preachers are called to say again what the church has forgotten, to bring to speech that which, from use or overuse, has become silent. What's lost is the gospel and, for a host of reasons, the gospel is lost again and again. But the good news is that the Good News is also discovered all over again. The gospel keeps rising from the dead, is made miraculously new each morning (Lamentations 3:22). God keeps redoing Easter. An old, old story becomes news.

Nobody needs to hear this word of homiletical encouragement more than us preachers. I look out upon my Sunday congregation and think: They aren't listening. They are the wrong people. This church is a mistake. The conditions for the gospel's renewal are not especially "propitious." But when have the conditions for the advent of Jesus Christ ever been right? He must make conditions right for preaching, or they will never be. He must make his own way into the world. He must rise from the dead every Sunday. He must enable fresh hearing. He must repeat himself. And, wonder of wonders, he does and, whenever he does, the gospel is redone.

In the Cloisters Museum in New York there is a medieval lintel—a stone over a doorway into an ancient church—that depicts a Palm Sunday procession. At the head of the procession is, of course, Jesus on a donkey. Just behind and around Jesus are children and disciples waving palm branches. They are dressed in the garb of the New Testament. But then, mingled in with them we note that there are contemporary medieval folk dressed in their Sunday best. A bishop and priests and townsfolk end the procession. Get it? We are walking through that doorway into church. We are taking our places in the Palm Sunday procession, marching behind Jesus, moving toward the future by taking our place in the past. We are enlisted into the very same parade. This is what happens, by the grace of God, when a sermon succeeds.

"How do I keep it fresh?" is finally not the right question for preachers to ask. "Keeping preaching fresh" is, in the end, not something we do as preachers. Faithful repetition is what we do; making it fresh is God's business. Our chief task as preachers is not to succeed but to try to preach again next Sunday, to keep at it, to keep saying the gospel, over and over again, confidently repetitious, sure in the conviction that God gives the gospel the hearing it deserves if we will stick with words akin to the God who sticks with us. We must be "Glad to be in church, one more time," as the old spiritual sings it. For now, there is only God-blessed trying.

A Sermon: Untimely Easter

When Jesus had crossed again in the boat to the other side, a great crowd gathered around him; and he was by the sea. Then one of the leaders of the synagogue named Jairus came and, when he saw him, fell at his feet and begged him repeatedly, "My little daughter is at the point of death. Come and lay your hands on her, so that she may be made well, and live." So he went with him.

And a large crowd followed him and pressed in on him. Now there was a woman who had been suffering from hemorrhages for twelve years. She had endured much under many physicians, and had spent all that she had; and she was no better, but rather grew worse. She had heard about Jesus, and came up behind him in the crowd and touched his cloak, for she said, "If I but touch his clothes, I will be made well." Immediately her hemorrhage stopped; and she felt in her body that she was healed of her disease. Immediately aware that power had gone forth from him, Jesus turned about in the crowd and said, "Who touched my clothes?" And his disciples said to him, "You see the crowd pressing in on you; how can you say, 'Who touched me?'" He looked all around to see who had done it. But the woman, knowing what had happened to her, came in fear and trembling, fell down before him, and told him the whole truth. He said to her, "Daughter, your faith has made you well; go in peace, and be healed of your disease."

> *While he was still speaking, some people came from the leader's house to say, "Your daughter is dead. Why trouble the teacher any further?" But overhearing what they said, Jesus said to the leader of the synagogue, "Do not fear, only believe." He allowed no one to follow him except Peter, James, and John, the brother of James. When they came to the house of the leader of the synagogue, he saw a commotion, people weeping and wailing loudly. When he had entered, he said to them, "Why do you make a commotion and weep? The child is not dead but sleeping." And they laughed at him. Then he put them all outside, and took the child's father and mother and those who were with him, and went in where the child was. He took her by the hand and said to her, "Talitha cum," which means, "Little girl, get up!" And immediately the girl got up and began to walk about (she was twelve years of age). At this they were overcome with amazement. He strictly ordered them that no one should know this, and told them to give her something to eat. (Mark 5:21-43)*

I know, I know. Easter is over. Yet still the church never quite gets over the inopportunity of Easter. We still keep being surprised that, whenever resurrected Jesus shows up, even in midsummer, the dead don't stay that way.

And I know there's no Easter in the Gospel of Mark. Mark ends abruptly with no resurrection appearances. There is a promise that hints of resurrection, but no resurrected Jesus in Mark. The last sentence of Mark, the response of the church to the good news that Jesus is raised from the dead? *Fear.* The women who came to the tomb in mourning left the empty tomb in fear.

Now, why would they be scared of Easter?

This absence of Easter in Mark has led some biblical scholars to say that Mark's gospel, the earliest of the gospels, is one long passion story, one long account of Jesus—faced with constant misunderstanding and opposition—walking grimly toward his cross. There's no resurrection in Mark, or so it seems.

Well, this Sunday we're barely in the middle of Mark's Gospel. Jesus has been working outside our boundaries, on the wrong side of the tracks, out over in Gentile territory. But now Jesus crosses back home, back to the faithful, the Bible-believers, back to us. Jesus is home among his own, home where he began his work, just a few months ago.

Home, as it turns out, is a place of death and dying. There is a poor woman who has been suffering sick for twelve years. A synagogue official has a dying daughter who is twelve years old. (Israel, I remind you, had twelve tribes. Jesus gathers twelve disciples. Is Mark about to tell us a story that challenges the inner circle, the insiders, us? That's opportune because anyone who would get out of bed, get dressed, and come to church has got to be a quintessential insider! All you insiders, listen up.)

Jesus is accosted by a church official who pleads, "My daughter's dying." Jesus and the official, Jarius, go home together. On the way the woman, who has been hemorrhaging for twelve years, who has used up her life savings on medical bills and ineffective therapies, pushes through the crowd and touches Jesus. We don't know her name. She is introduced as a woman who is sick and has suffered much at the hands of doctors. Her sickness has named her, dominated her, consumed her, which is what dying tends to do.

"If I could just touch him, I'd be healed," she says. She would have an identity other than her sickness.

And she is healed. This woman, enslaved by sickness for over a decade, as good as dead, named by her dying, is healed, brought back from the dead. We don't know what theology she adhered to, or if she was active in the Synagogue. All we know is that she reached out, touched Jesus, and received resurrection, just by touching him.

Now this healing-on-the-way is wonderful but by the time Jesus gets to Jairus' house, it's all over. His beloved little girl is dead. The weeping and wailing tell the sad news. Unfortunately Jesus has come too late to help the little girl.

"Why are you making such a fuss?" Jesus asks. "Mr. Lord of Life is here!" And the crowd turns from tears and mourning to mocking laughter. "Sure, like she's only asleep!" Nice timing, Jesus. You're late.

And Jesus touches her, announces, "It's time to get up!" And the derisive laughter becomes shocked wonder. Jesus' disciples, the ones gathered in this house of death, were "astounded." And even though it's not Easter, even though it's the dead of summer, whenever Jesus shows up, it's Easter. They were astounded.

We still are.[41]

Here is the church, the insiders, us, all adjusted to death. Stoic resignation is about the best our theology can deliver. Mainline, Protestant Christians, in our membership malaise, console ourselves with, "Everybody's losing members." Amen. Decline is prevalent. Amen. Death is normal, we say with a knowing smirk. Declining birthrates among liberal, mainline Protestants lead to declining congregations. Simple as that. Church growth? It's a gimmick, a simplistic quick fix best suited for less progressive and well-educated congregations, we say with a progressive sneer.

"Do you think my son will ever get over his drug addiction?" she asked me. And I, as her enlightened pastor, replied, in love, "Recovery from heroin? What are the chances of that? Get serious. Get real." Mocking laughter is the way a sophisticated, stoic disposition refers to talk of Easter.

That expression, "Get real," translated into today's Scripture means "adjust to death." So when this desperate father presses in upon Jesus, when this poor, harried woman reaches toward Jesus, the home folks react with a sardonic smile. Jesus responds by offering some sufferers new life, hope, a future. Jesus doesn't say some magical incantation, doesn't offer some esoteric technique. Jesus just shows up. He allows the woman just to touch him. He speaks to the dead girl. And there is resurrection.

Jesus commands, "Little girl, get up!" Arise! Be resurrected! Jesus apparently resuscitated only three throughout his ministry: Jairus' daughter, the widow's son at Nain (Luke 7:11-17), and Lazarus (John 11:1-44). Why didn't he raise all the dead whom he encountered in his journeys?

Of course, the reasons are known only to Jesus, but perhaps we are not to see Jesus as a spectacularly, though sporadically, successful doctor (unlike the "diverse physicians" who have plagued the poor, bleeding woman). Rather Jesus is a revolutionary, a challenger of the status quo, a teacher who teaches us how to overturn the world, a subversive who has invaded deadly enemy territory (which happens to be his own homeland) in order to wrench it from the grip of Death, conquer it and hold it for his own.

Sometimes biblical scholars point out that what we have here, in this raising from the dead, is more precisely "resuscitation" rather than "resurrection" since, though Jesus raised these people from the dead, they eventually died. The resurrection, they note, is participation in God's eternal life, not a temporary respite from death.

Yet I think it's fair to read this as Mark's rendition of the meaning of resurrection. Jesus is the one who is raised from the dead. That would be wonder enough. But wonder of wonders, Jesus is the one who raises others from the dead. Whenever Jesus shows up, even in the eighth chapter, long before the time for Easter, the dead are raised. Mark just can't wait until the end to tell these miraculous stories because, with Jesus, the time is always right for resurrection. By telling these stories here, resurrection gets political—a political challenge to the mocking bystanders and to the stupefied disciples. Who gets to name what's real, what's really going on in the world and when? Jesus refuses deferentially to wait until a more auspicious time to go on the attack. Whenever Jesus walks into town, even when he is on the way, even in the dead of summer, the time is right for resurrection. Whenever Jesus commands, "Get up!" or allows somebody just to reach out and touch him, then, even if it's July, hot, and dry, it's Easter.

When I was in conversation with Marcus Borg of the Jesus Seminar, Marcus asked me, "Why do you need a supernaturally resurrected body of Jesus to make your faith work?"

And I responded, in love, "Marcus, I don't need a resurrected Jesus. Come to think of it, I'm not sure I want a resurrected Jesus. In fact, if I got one, it would be real nuisance for me, personally. I've got a good life, I've figured out how to work the world, on the whole, to the advantage of me and my friends and family. My health is good, everybody close to me is doing fine. I have the illusion that I'm in control, that I am making a so-significant contribution to help Jesus that I may be eternal on my own. No, I don't need a bodily resurrected Jesus. In fact, if I ever got one, my life would only become much more difficult."

When the possibility of resurrection really comes through to you, when the rumor that something's afoot becomes a reality for you, well, you can see why the women were scared that first Easter.

At the Monday morning clergy coffee hour, one of the young pastors excitedly reported some rather spectacular growth in the past year at a megachurch in another town.

"It's really a miracle," he said.

One of the older, wiser pastors at the table responded with a chuckle, "It's no miracle. That guy has gathered a little group of admirers around himself. He's not made a church; he's made a personality cult to himself."

Another laughed, "He's such a showman! Have you ever seen him perform on Sunday morning? He's just got a good act that attracts a crowd."

Mocking, cynical laughter is the way that death keeps control and attempts to keep Mr. Life at bay.

When I heard the size of the projected budget for the coming year (I was away on vacation when the finance committee voted), I laughed. "Let me get this straight. A church that is this year ten percent behind in collections for the budget is going to have an increase of ten percent for next year's budget? Get real!"

Still, the lay leadership persisted. (Laity are often unrealistic in their expectations.) My contribution to the fall stewardship campaign was frequently to smirk, "You'll never make that budget."

Three Sundays into the campaign, the stewardship chair made his Sunday report. "We've had something of a miracle here, folks," he said. "Just three weeks into the campaign we have met our goal."

Spontaneous applause.

He continued, "Which is all the more amazing because next year's budget is ten percent more than this year's."

Widespread applause.

"Now, as I recall, there was someone who said, when we started this venture, 'You will never make that budget.' Who was it who said that? Help me. I can't rightly remember. Who said, 'You will never make that budget'?"

"Sit down and shut up," I said, in love.

I don't know where there is a shadow in your life. I don't know what dead end you are dealing with. I don't know what you may have lost or where you might be hemorrhaging. I do know that Jesus is the Lord of Life, that he is master, even over death, anyplace, anytime.

I'm a United Methodist bishop, so a big part of my job is to send pastors to churches. Some of the churches are so difficult, or so dead and deadly, that sometimes a pastor doesn't want to be sent there. The pastors are afraid that they might catch what the church has got. One of my District Superintendents was telling me that a pastor was resisting his appointment, protesting, "That church is hopeless! There is no way to turn around the downward slide there. It's dead! I'll just die if I'm sent there!"

The District Superintendent defended our appointment by saying, "Well, I'll tell the bishop what you said. But I need to warn you, this bishop truly believes that the resurrection is a fact. He actually believes that Jesus bodily, really, truthfully rose from the dead on Easter. He even thinks that Jesus still does. So you need to know that when you say something like 'That church is dead,' it really doesn't mean a thing to the bishop because he thinks Easter is true."

It was a great compliment, probably undeserved. Still, I couldn't help thinking to myself, "Imagine that? After sixty years of trying, this church has almost made me a Christian."

CHAPTER FOUR

TIME DISRUPTED

Sam Wells says, "God gives us all we need."[1] What? Considering the inadequacies of my church, the multiple shortcomings within me as a preacher, it's a stretch to believe that we indeed have all that is required. Most of my lectures and sermons begin with the assumption of lack, the supposition of paucity and a want of faith—"Nine Reasons You Are Not Really a Christian Though You Thought You Were When You Came to Church This Morning." If the church cannot exhaust the resources of the Kingdom, does that also apply to the church's time in the pulpit?

Jesus told stories of divine abundance: seed that, though much of it was lost in the sowing, produced abundant, miraculous, hundredfold harvest (Mark 4:26-29). Then there was the tiny, seemingly insignificant mustard seed that grew to be a large, bird-supporting shrub (Mark 4:30-32). When a quandary arises about a depletion of alcohol at a post-wedding bash, Jesus produced 180 gallons of wine, even though just a few six packs would have sufficed (John 2). And when he fed the hungry multitude, the wonder was not just that Jesus produced enough nourishment to satisfy; the miracle was that a huge amount of food was left over (Mark 6:30-44).

I know. It is more true to the Greek in John 1:5 to say that the "light shines in the darkness, and the darkness did not overcome it." But I find more true to pastoral experience the old Authorized Version's "the light shineth in darkness; and the darkness comprehendeth it not." With Scripture's fecundity, even slight mistranslations are rewarding—with Jesus there was a surplus of light, a surfeit of dawn, luminosity in such abundance that the darkness found its brilliance incomprehensible. The good news for us preachers is that in spite of the efforts of modernity, the world has not yet found the means for disenchanting the world. The world is not, thank God, godforsaken.

Over the long haul, we preachers learn to cling to the belief that the Christian faith is a self-renewing resource. Our homiletical failures cannot outdo the abundance of God. Because of the loquacious nature of the true and living God, there is always something else to be said, more light yet to be shed next Sunday. (Who among us can claim to have read, much less digested or proclaimed, the whole of Scripture?) We need not add to God's revelation, make some helpful contribution to God's self-disclosure. There is already more than we'll do justice to in a lifetime of sermons. There is always something left unsaid about the Trinity, even after the longest of homilies. We could go on, eternally. All sermons are too short.

John Calvin argues that even the most ignorant pagan knows a great deal about the true God simply because of the abundance of God. God has left signs, traces, and evidence all over the world that even the most obtuse among us cannot ignore.[2] How can Calvin say that even pagans have knowledge of God when they have no Scripture, no church, to say nothing of preachers? Calvin makes this claim out of his confidence in the nature of the Trinity. It is God's nature to reveal, not to hide, but rather to show, to divulge, constantly to communicate. Luther made a big deal of the *deus absconditus*, the tendency of God to be coy, but not Calvin. The whole earth is full of the knowledge of God because of who God is, said Calvin.

> The Way that can be told of is not an unvarying way;
> The names that can be named are not unvarying names.[3]

Thus begins the *Tao Te Ching*. The divine is apophatic, ineffable, unspeakable, or it is not divine—any way that can be spoken is not really *the* way. Christianity takes a decidedly different view of spirituality. True, the divine is ineffable, incapable of human analogy or description. But the ineffability is because only God can speak of God. In preaching to a listening congregation, God speaks. Unlike the *Tao*, God tells us God's name (Exod 3:13) then repeatedly tells us the way. Our God tells us all we need to know in order to live the abundant life, here, now.

The modern world has overdone the idea of a hidden God in an attempt to keep God quiet. We take our doubt too seriously, unaware of the stake that modernity has in convincing us that God is mute. Indeed, as I read the classical theology of Calvin, Luther, Irenaeus, Aquinas, or Barth, the major difference between them and the contemporary theology that I read (and much that I write!) is their conviction that God is abundantly revelatory. Though Luther appreciates the *deus absconditus*, he also seems at one with Paul in 2 Corinthians that Christ is the full revelation of God among those who heretofore did not know God. Now we are given the gift of being able to see God "with unveiled faces" (2 Cor 3:17-18). That which was once incomprehensible "mystery" is now mysteriously revealed (Col 1:25-28). The purposes of God have now been made plain. "*And all of us* [not just us preachers], with unveiled faces, seeing the glory of the Lord . . . , are being transformed . . . this comes from the Lord, the Spirit" (2 Cor 3:18, emphasis mine). There is more than enough revelation in Christ to go around.

Although the modern world has attempted to convince us that we are writing our own stories, the Christian faith keeps asserting that we live in stories that we did not write. We preachers have the privilege of talking people into a world where much is afoot and some Other is the author of the true story of what is going on in us and in the world.[4] As Paul told his congregation, "You are a letter of Christ, prepared by us, written not with ink but with the Spirit of the living God" (2 Cor 3:3). God gives us all we need. By the grace of God, there is a surfeit of sermon material.

The Trinity is not only abundantly loquacious but also so complex that no matter how much we say about God, there is a surplus of meaning yet to be said. Because of this triune largess, it takes time to assimilate Jesus. This dominical complexity, this excess of meaning in Jesus, is one reason we learn the Scriptures' meaning only over time. Preachers don't really find our "voice" until a few years into the practice of preaching because preachers are talking about a subject—the triune God—who resists ready descriptions. It is the nature of the Holy Spirit always to slip through the hands of even our most astute characterizations of the Holy Spirit.

And yet, as we have noted, the modern world adores simple descriptions and limited characterizations. Modern methods of knowing are inherently minimalist and reductionistic. When I was taught historical criticism of Scripture, I was told to try to think about the text objectively, that is, through the practice of a sort of intentional amnesia. I was urged to strip myself of all preconceptions, to suppress my imaginative capacities, and to try to think about the text following this simple method of applied historical criticism.

At best, historical criticism kept us from arriving at the meaning of a text too soon, imposing our expectations on the text before the text could speak for itself. The result, however, has been generations of students who are fearful of finding any meaning in the text at all, listeners to scripture whose method almost prohibits them from hearing anything really shocking and life changing in Scripture. No wonder that preachers were among the first to notice the prejudices and limitations of the historical-critical method.

How different is the impoverished modern approach to revelation when compared with classical modes of biblical interpretation. John Calvin, a master hermeneut, marveled that even when we sleep, even in our dreams, this relentlessly revelatory God talks, gets through to us, making even our times of unconsciousness occasions for revelation by a Holy Spirit who works the night shift, a God who talks on into the night, even when we are not trying to listen, even when we yearn for silence, especially then.[5] We thought that in sleep we were unconscious when in truth God is raising us, through nocturnal conversation, to a higher, deeper consciousness.

Rather than submit to God's surfeit and complexity and to allow preaching to be miraculous, we preachers still hope that there is some method, some technique that will insure that preaching simply works. An important ethical quality demanded of preachers is the willingness to submit to and to be intimate with the biblical text (rather than, as historical criticism tended to teach us, to dominate and to distance ourselves from the text). In order to perform the text, we must submit to its authority over us over time. We must be willing to be seduced.

Biblical interpretation is an art rather than a science. Submission, with more than a touch of playfulness, is required of us in the art of biblical interpretation. Any good artist submits to the medium of the art. Wallace Bacon, a performance theorist, writes that when reading a poem in public, "The performer who cares more about pleasing an audience than about enactment of the poem will endanger the whole poetic experience . . . [there must be in the performer] an act of communion with the poem; if the reader communes with the audience but not with the poem, the audience is likely to come away with spirits unfed."[6] The same is true for biblical interpretation for preaching.

A major motivation for the historical-critical method of interpreting Scripture was to give us preachers a trouble-free method whereby we attained a sure and certain word to speak, a set of ideas shorn of all historical contingency, a message that was beyond the scriptural context, news that was sure to be heard anywhere and by anyone, proclamation that could be constructed by any preacher regardless of the preacher's gifts.

It didn't work.

Calvin was deeply convinced that the form and operation of Scripture are "derived from the character of the divine speaker." That is why the prophets and apostles, said Luther, have "a queer way of talking" and Calvin said the prophets speak not from "their own genius or any of those talents which conciliate the faith of the hearers; nor do they insist on arguments from reason" but rather they speak out of the abundance that God has given them.[7] All preaching in God's name is miraculous. Preaching "works," not because of the abilities of preacher or the hearers but only because the Holy Spirit miraculously makes it work. When faced with the impossibility of preaching, the ludicrousness of Almighty God speaking through us preachers, Barth replied that if God spoke through Balaam's jackass (Num 22: 28-30), God was surely free to condescend to speak through preachers.

Why do I believe this with all my heart? I believe because I've witnessed God speaking in spite of me (to spite me?) on so many Sundays. I expect God to speak through my best sermons, the ones on which I've worked hard and well. But sometimes the Trinity takes a sort of perverse delight in not speaking through those well-wrought homiletical products in order to make some kind of divine point. Perhaps the point that God is making is that only God can preach. I do not intend to provide justification for poor preparation among lazy preachers. However, I am here celebrating that God is not obligated to speak through my good homiletical practice nor is God's vocative activity limited by my bad sermons. Despite my compulsive preparation, or lack of it, wonder of wonders, *God does preach*.[8] All preaching is *ek theou*, "from God" (2 Cor 2:17). God gives us all we need.

It is of the nature of a literary work as complex and demanding as the Bible, with its Old and New Testaments, to be understood cumulatively, over time. To understand Scripture we must acquire wisdom, prudence, self-discipline, and self-knowledge. This makes preaching one of the few occupations where someone usually improves with age. It takes time to cultivate, stoke, fund, and fuel the imagination. As Auden said, you don't have to be a poet to be a Christian, but it sure helps. Neither prudence nor poetic imagination comes overnight. Older preachers, perhaps because they have been shocked or befuddled by the oddness of reality so often are possibly blessed with a more fertile imagination than young preachers who think they actually learned to master Scripture in seminary.

Marilynne Robinson is a brilliant contemporary author. And yet, she confesses befuddlement when faced with Scripture, which is "always new to me" because it is "almost entirely elusive." Robinson declares,

> I know many other books very well and I flatter myself that I understand them—even books by people like Augustine and Calvin. But I do not understand the Bible. I study theology as one would watch a solar eclipse in a shadow. In church, the devout old custom persists of merely repeating verses of one or another luminous fragment, . . . By grace of my abiding ignorance, it is always new to me. I am never not instructed. . . . The text itself always remains almost entirely elusive. So I must come back to hear it again; in the old phrase, to have it opened for me again.[9]

In the *Common Lectionary*, the story of Jesus blessing the children (Mark 10:2-16) is placed with Job 1:1, 2:1-10. For five or six times through the lectionary I had always focused on the Gospel, Mark 10, without any reference in my sermon to Job. But my last time through I suddenly saw the connection that heretofore had eluded me: the Jesus who reaches out and embraces weak, dependent children is one with the God who finally came back to weak, dependent Job. Neither Mark nor Job, in these episodes, "explains" why God draws near to the weak and the dispossessed. (Scripture is almost never in the explanatory mood. Scripture specializes in the declarative, the indicative mood.) Neither the vulnerable little children nor the ravaged, vulnerable Job get an explanation; they get embraced by a God who tends to come closer as we get smaller. It took me forty years of reading the Gospel to hear that message through the church's bundling of two initially disparate biblical texts, neither of which explicitly mentions the other.

Preaching Present Tense

In her book, *Marking Time: Preaching Biblical Stories in the Present Tense*, Barbara K. Lundblad[10] recalls how, as a theology student, she heard Frederick Buechner give the 1977 Beecher Lectures at Yale Divinity School. Buechner began by recounting Lyman Beecher's inaugural lectures a hundred years earlier. Buechner told how Beecher had not been feeling well the night before the 1872 lectures. He went into some detail about how Beecher began writing the lectures in his hotel room in the middle of the night in New Haven.

The next thing the listeners knew, Buechner was talking about another insomniac, Pontius Pilate, as if Pilate were a contemporary of Beecher's or maybe a contemporary with Buechner. Pontius Pilate lit a cigarette. He looked at the picture on the wall of his children. Pilate began thinking about his wife. Oops, Pilate cut himself while shaving that morning.

The preacher adeptly, rather slyly, moved from the nineteenth century, back to the first century, or is it forward into the late twentieth century? Without warning, the hearers are faced with two historical figures contemporized. Lundblad said it was a disarming, invigorating experience that helped direct her own preaching vocation. She knew then and there that she wanted to be the sort of preacher who moves the gospel into the present tense.

Preachers love to mix up the tenses of verbs. In their "Notes on the Translation of the Greek Tenses" in the *New American Standard Bible*, the translators explain:

> In regard to the use of the historic present, the Board recognized that in some contexts the present tense seems more unexpected and unjustified to the English reader than the past tense would have been. But Greek authors frequently used the present tense for the sake of heightened vividness, thereby transporting their readers in imagination to the actual scene at the time of occurrence. However the Board felt that it would be wise to change these historic presents into English past tenses. Therefore verbs marked with an asterisk (*) represent historical presents in the Greek which have been translated with an English past tense in order to conform to modern usage.[11]

Why on earth would the translators feel the need to make these modifications in the original Greek? Perhaps the compilers of Scripture actually wanted Scripture sometimes to sound "unexpected and unjustified." We preachers have a propensity to move, in our sermons, from the past tense of Scripture into the present tense of our congregations' lives—which could be a major purpose of preaching.

Preachers Raise the Dead

John Calvin (in his meditations on God the Creator) marveled at the "manifold agility of the soul which enables it to . . . join the past and the present, to retain the memory of things heard long ago, to conceive of whatever it chooses by the help of the imagination."[12] For Calvin, our imaginative ability to join past and present, to make past present is evidence of the divine within the human. I share Calvin's wonder that we can speak and think in past, present, and future tenses. Our language is inherently temporal, arising out of some present that is now past, but also thrusting us toward the future. Our speech can represent to us something that has ceased to be and it can also create something that was not before it was uttered. Words make world.

We only speak what the past has given us, in words we did not invent ourselves, and yet, in speaking we give ourselves a different future. Language is in time but it also is the major means that we have of transcending time. Words contribute, construct, and offer us a future that is alternative to the meager one we would have had without the utterance. It is only through words that I can have a "past" or a "future."[13] "Jesus Christ is Lord" is a performative utterance. In saying "Jesus Christ is Lord," Jesus becomes Lord, now. Time is undone and thereby something is done, reality is changed. In regard to what is real, it's words all the way down.

Thus almost every statement I make is a kind of "resurrection," a daily experience of kenotic dying to the past, miraculously rising in the present, and dramatically moving toward a future I could not have had without the words. Christians name this dynamic as Easter. Thus we preachers, in our sermons, allow God to perform, to make things live, and present that which was past or absent, even dead, as now.[14] (I think this is close to Paul's meaning when he says that the Holy Spirit is the "first installment" [2 Cor 1:22]. The Holy Spirit's vivification of our words in today's sermon is a preview, a promise, first installment of the general resurrection that is to come.) The Bible is not some ancient, ossified document; it is a talking book, an instrument in the Holy Spirit's rich repertoire of means of changing the world, of making God present tense. Preachers raise the dead, sort of.

In *Amusing Ourselves to Death*,[15] Neil Postman notes that in the current age there is a marked difference in the way people pay attention. The main factor in this change has been television. Communication gets speeded up in TV, quickly depicted, giving us the illusion that it takes little time to understand complex realities. Television gives the illusion that we are experiencing something in "real time," that is, in the present moment. But of course we are not.

For those of us who communicate outside of television, to people whose consciousness has been formed by television, this has significance because of the illusion that television creates. Wendell Berry has a poem in which he tells about a man going on vacation, seeing his vacation through a camera. He takes pictures of everything under the illusion that, through film, he could forever remember his vacation, seeing all the places he had been. Sadly, he would never, ever be in any of the pictures. He would have pictures of his vacation, but always without him. The camera has given the illusion of eternality to our experience and yet in a way it has robbed us of experience; we are not there, we are never, ever really *there*.[16]

When we preachers interpret Scripture, we are doing more than objectively examining a snapshot of God. We are offering ourselves to an active, free conversation between living partners.[17] We are enticing the congregation to climb a perilous path with us. We are nervously unwrapping a ticking bomb. This is of course counter to the view of Schleiermacher, who said that the purpose of interpretation is to "understand the text at first as well and then even better than its author."[18] The biblical interpreter, in Schleiermacher's characterization, attempts to reproduce what was in the mind of the original biblical writer. Interpretation is simple re-presentation of an author's past meaning into the interpreter's present consciousness. First figure out the minimal meaning of the text in the past, and then deliver what's left as what the text ought to mean in the present. The Bible is a photo album, a kind of archive of what God once meant to people and the preacher must labor to make it mean something today. (How typical of the modern world to frame the matter this way: interpretation is a problem of time. The modern interpreter takes a superior position to the historical text by delivering the meaning of the text "even better than its author.")

Schleiermacher's view of hermeneutics reigned until Hans-Georg Gadamer's great *Truth and Method*. Gadamer believed that interpretation is an engaging, potentially transforming conversation between interpreter and text. Every text "must be understood at every moment, in every concrete situation, in a new and different way. Understanding here is always application," said Gadamer.[19] Interpretation occurs when a text breaks into the life of an individual or a group and, in breaking in at that particular time and place, the text itself is amplified in that interpretation. Interpretation entails transformation. The text changes the interpreter and the interpreter changes the text. The path of interpretation is not straight, not forward, but circular, back and forth. We question a text, but a text also questions us. There is a real sense in which we don't have the same Bible that our spiritual forebears read. We serve a living Christ, not a dead text.

For example, I've preached at least four sermons on Revelation 5:11-14 (Easter 3 in *Lectionary* C). My earliest sermon notes that, when the battle for the cosmos is over, when God wins, the Supreme Ruler is none other than a slaughtered lamb. What does that tell you about the world's destiny? My second sermon settled upon the verse "every creature in heaven and on earth and under the earth and in the sea, and all that is in them, singing" (5:13). That sermon took an ecological theme, speaking of the eschatological healing of all creation and God's promised restoration. Every creature shall participate in God's promised salvation. My third sermon was interspersed with music from the choir and characterized this earthly existence as "one long choir rehearsal" so that we might learn to sing the song today that one day we shall sing to God forever. My fourth pass at Revelation 5 marveled at the "myriad" creatures before the throne of the Lamb, the "thousands of thousands" and took a sort of universal salvation approach to the text. Salvation appears to be not for a few, but for myriads. Looking over those four sermons, it is as if I'm not talking about the same text, which in a way, I'm not. It is the same text displaying its thickness and its richness to the church as well as the same church displaying its diversity over time to the text. Thank God—for those of us who are called to preach for more than four decades—Scripture is multivalent.[20]

Harvard's James L. Kugel has shown that early biblical interpreters saw the entire Bible as a "divinely given text," a rich, though mysterious, literature that provoked constant discovery of hidden meanings.[21] Modernity attempted to reduce Scripture. Modern biblical study, says Kugel (a Jew) is indebted to Spinoza, who stressed that Scripture mainly means what it literally means. The simple, literal reading is to be preferred over the symbolic, metaphorical meaning. Scripture, said Spinoza, is not eternally true but rather is historically true, true for some people living at a certain time but without much relevance for our time. Spinoza thus paved the way for historical criticism's treatment of Scripture as a source of information about ancient cultures. Modernity rendered us into Scripture's examiners rather than Scripture's hearers. Scripture as the medium for a living, speaking theological Agent is lost in favor of Scripture as a kind of archeological dig.[22] Kugel gives the somber verdict that "modern biblical scholarship and traditional Judaism are and must remain completely irreconcilable." Could the same be said of modern biblical scholarship and Christianity?

I find myself in the same situation as P. T. Forsyth, who said, in his 1907 Lyman Beecher Lectures, that although as a scholar he agreed with the historical critics who did not believe in "verbal inspiration" of Scripture, as a practicing preacher he had so often witnessed the fecundity and activity of Scripture that it was a struggle for him not to believe in the verbal inspiration of Scripture![23]

Bonhoeffer marvels at how the church's encounters with Scripture

> force everyone who wants to hear to put himself, or to allow himself to be found, where God has acted once and for all for the salvation of men. We become a part of what once took place for our salvation. Forgetting and losing ourselves, we, too, pass through the Red Sea, through the desert, across the Jordan into the promised land. With Israel we fall into doubt and unbelief and through punishment and repentance experience again God's help and faithfulness. All this is not mere reverie but holy, godly reality. We are torn out of our own existence and set down in the midst of the holy history of God on earth. There God deals with us, and there he still deals with us, our needs and our sins, in judgment and grace. It is not that God is the spectator and sharer of our present life, howsoever important that is; but rather that we are the reverent listeners and participants in God's action in the sacred story, the history of the Christ on earth. And only in so far as we are there, is God with us today also.[24]

For all of Scripture's revelatory virtues, Barth said that even Scripture is not primary but rather secondary divine communication. Divine communication is proclamation from God. Scripture is a kind of deposit of what is left over after the lightening bolt of divine proclamation. Scripture is the residue of what once was proclaimed on human lips as preaching. In preaching, Scripture lives, we are thrust into that primal divine proclamation. In preaching, Scripture's account of revelation to someone, somewhere in time becomes news, now. Therefore, for Barth, preaching is primary, even to Scripture, for as Paul says,[25] it is the sound of proclamation on human lips that saves, not its appearance on the printed page.[26] Faith comes through hearing.

Preaching is used by God not only to be present tense but also to render presence. Karl Barth asserted that Christian theology must honor the distinction between "primary objectivity"—God's knowledge of God's self—and "secondary objectivity"—God's presence to God's creatures that can only be indirect, through some finite reality (such as Scripture or another human being, or even the person Jesus of Nazareth). Then Barth stunningly asserts that this available "secondary objectivity" (Scripture, preaching, Jesus Christ) is not one bit less truth than the primary reality. When the Creator is present to us humans—as words, as the Word, the crucified Jew from Nazareth—God is truthfully, really present, though in a form that is graciously available to the creature. There is no difference in degree. The God we meet in preaching really is the God who is. There is, in Jesus Christ, no God lurking behind the God who greets us in Christ. God is with us. God's true goodness with us in Jesus Christ is God present and God's relational presence repeated. Preaching, as the proclamation by God of God, is presence of God.

> My word . . . that goes out from my mouth;
>   it shall not return to me empty,
> but it shall accomplish that which I purpose,
>   and succeed in the thing for which I sent it. (Isa 55:11)

This vivid, vivifying conviction of God's real presence in Christ, repeated in preaching, led Barth to announce the end of all "religion." We need not have rituals, practices, institutions to enable us—through our thought and our action—to climb up to God, to ascend to some future level of insight where we are not now, because God has become present to us now. Presence is a gift that only God can give, and in preaching, God abundantly gives.

Thus Walter Brueggemann says that the question before us preachers is not the vague, metaphysical speculation "Is God's word powerful?" Rather, in regard to God's word the question is: dare we embrace the word's contemporaneity, God's "present-tense struggle among us"? Brueggemann asks, "Can the synagogue and the church, the communities committed to this prophetic claim, do the hard, demanding intellectual, rhetorical work that will construe the world according to this memory and this discourse?"[27]

I would characterize Brueggemann's question as not "Can God become present?" but rather "Do we preachers have the guts to name the world, the present world, the world we've got, as God's world, here, now?" This suggests that the historical—the temptation to make God's word past tense—is always a threat to bold, present-tense speech. Brueggemann also leads me to wonder if we preachers are tempted to cast the hermeneutical task as one of moving from what was past to the present because we are caught in a web of commitments to—and we profit from—the old order. Thus we unwittingly become servants to the (now that Jesus has come) discredited, dethroned old world as a means of evading Jesus' new world.

Jesus somehow managed to preach the reign of God as a future advent that we anticipate and as a present-tense event that is now. David Buttrick calls this present-future orientation "the most important distinction" that is to be made about the preaching of Jesus, this invitation by Jesus to "step into the new order ahead of time."[28] Eschatology keeps pressing us toward that fresh experience of future that also freshens our preaching. In preaching we are always talking about an eschatological reality that is here, now but also "ahead of time." Of course, one way the world defends itself against such claims is to tell us that we are talking unrealistically, describing our fantasy of the future rather than the facts that are now.

Preaching Again

Most of us preachers learn various techniques, mostly rhetorical, to keep our preaching fresh. Among those that I utilize in my own ministry:

- We use the *Common Lectionary* as a source for our sermons. By being pushed into a wider array of scriptures than if we had been left to our own devices, by being forced to preach on texts chosen by the church rather than texts chosen by ourselves, preachers keep being challenged by Scripture in fresh ways. The *Common Lectionary* helps keep preaching fresh by driving us to preach what we've been told to preach.

- Our lives, as preachers, are constantly changing and developing. God is never done with us. So change in us becomes a stimulus for change in what we preach.

- Scripture is so diverse that, in our speaking the scriptures in sermons, we modulate, vary our tone and presentation as much as the scriptures themselves. The literary richness of the scriptures is an impetus for freshness.

- We develop disciplines like reading and weekly study to renew our minds, to put us in conversation with other preachers and in order to keep stoking our creativity and imagination. I keep a book of poetry at my bedside and keep a novel close by to challenge my laziness with language and to give me a better mind than I would have had without being friends with Thomas Mann and Flannery O'Connor.

- Pastoral visitation and the constant human contact within our parish work keep raising new questions and giving us new insights that are derived from our parishioners. You wouldn't believe what God is capable of doing among ordinary people in South Carolina. On many a Thursday afternoon, stuck in my sermon preparation, I would venture forth to visit parishioners. Rarely would I return to my study empty-handed.

- We go out from the cozy confines of the initiated and the well-formed in the faith (most church folks) and evangelize, gathering a new group of listeners who have new and more interesting spiritual dilemmas and require more indoctrination and explanation than our present congregations. New believers are a stimulus to those of us who can't remember when we were not Christian.

- We intentionally focus on that scripture that we have always found to be obtuse, boring, or offensive and take as our challenge to preach on an odd text, discovering that the resulting sermon is more interesting than a sermon on scripture that we like.

- Our boredom with our own preaching can be a gift that stimulates us to try out new styles and different methods of homiletic presentation in an effort not to bore ourselves to death.[29]

- When we tire of talking to the same people about the same gospel, we shake the dust off our feet, try to repress the memory of our homiletical failures among them, and ask the bishop to move us to a different congregation.

While all these pastoral methods for renewal can be somewhat invigorating, none of them stirs us preachers like talk about a true and living God like the Trinity. I repeat myself: refreshed preaching is not primarily the result of astutely applied homiletic method. Refreshed preaching is the gift of faithful talk about, and prayerful talk with, and abundant talk by a living God. The renewal of preaching is Jesus' job, not ours.

God, in the power of the Holy Spirit, is the key to everything. In a way, this book has been an extended meditation on the relationship of pneumatology to preaching. The Holy Spirit may be the most neglected aspect of homiletics today. Many of the hermeneutical methods and sermon construction strategies that we learned in seminary are themselves unintentional means of warding off intrusions by the Holy Spirit. Much of our apologetic intent is an unintended means of doing God's work for God. Some of our historical criticism of Scripture is a way of indefinitely postponing the question "Is it true?" As Gadamer noted, the modern world thinks it is using methodology to get to the truth when often method is the means of avoiding encounters with the truth. It isn't a sermon until the Holy Spirit enters, speaks, intrudes, and makes it a sermon.

In Harold Ramis's endlessly rewatchable movie *Groundhog Day*, Bill Murray plays the most superficial of men engaged in the most inane of jobs (reporting the weather). One drab morning in a dull Pennsylvania town he awakes to the radio blaring Sonny and Cher's whining rendition of their most pointless song, "I Got You Babe." He then plods through his day, encountering a group of wearisome people along the way.

The next morning the radio awakens him at the same time, with the same song—Sonny and Cher all over again—and the same weather report, which he thinks a bit odd. But things become even stranger as he stumbles through exactly the same day with the same boring people as yesterday. And then the next day and the next. After the twentieth repetition of the same pointless day, Murray realizes he is in hell. In a number of vain attempts to end it all, he tries to commit suicide, leaping from a building, falling in front of a speeding truck. But after each attempt, he awakens the next day to the same song, same day, Sonny and Cher again. He then engages in a life of crime, doing all those things that he was reluctant to do before his days became gruesome repetition. After even the worst of crimes, he awakens the next morning to "I Got You Babe" and begins his day all over again.

Realizing that he has no way of escaping the humdrum of the same day hellishly repeated, he launches into a program of self-improvement. He takes up piano. He memorizes poetry. He makes love like a Frenchman. He transforms himself into an interesting person and, in the process, the people around him, for whom he once had such contempt, become interesting to him. Only then is he freed from the wheel of the eternal return.

Murray extricates himself from hellish repetition through heroic self-improvement. This is the story that the modern world (and Joel Osteen's sermons) thinks it is now living—take charge of your life and transform yourself into someone worth loving and use your time to make a life worth living. Christians believe another story than that of *Groundhog Day*. A life worth living we believe to be a gift of God, time worth having we believe to be solely the work of the Holy Spirit. The unexpected, even unwanted, intrusions of the Holy Spirit keep disrupting our socially sanctioned narratives of progress or decline, suggest another story at work beyond our optimism or our pessimism. We discover, in the eschatological stories of the Christian faith, that we are part of a larger narrative whose ending is more than we could produce on our own.

I was a preacher in a university chapel for twenty years. In two decades in academia, I rarely made anyone really angry with what I wrote, or with a comment I made during a counseling session. Their anger was reserved for my sermons. To be sure, the evocation of anger is not always a test for faithful preaching, though resentment was the usual response to the preaching of Jesus. Still, their rage was revealing. A fairly typical angry rejoinder to my sermons was "You shouldn't talk like that in front of students."

I note in passing that Socrates was also criticized for "corrupting the youth," though through other means.

Give my university listeners credit. They knew. Preaching is frequently used by God to assault the status quo, to disrupt our time, to rip off from the kids the future that their parents offered to them through the mechanism of the modern, first-rate, selective university. Preaching doesn't necessarily aim to evoke anger, elicit resistance, and provoke disruption. It doesn't have to. Just talking about and speaking for a God like the Trinity will be disruptive aplenty. It's the typical effect a God like this has on people like us. It's what the Holy Spirit ordinarily does.

We are, each of us, a work in progress; not our progress, of course, but rather products of the Holy Spirit. When hands are laid upon us at baptism, and the Holy Spirit is invoked, the trouble begins. God is neither a safe principle nor a noble idea; God is dangerously, intimately personified. As Bonhoeffer said, preaching *is the Christ himself walking through his congregation as the word.* And sometimes he stalks or runs.

God is a living, speaking, abundantly revealing, encroaching, frenetic, frequently disrupting presence who, as with Jacob, sometimes in a sermon wrestles us to the ground, half kills us, blesses us and commands us, and then steals back into the night as we limp away—when all we wanted was a civil conversation. Karl Barth was fond of saying, "God never rests." God is always God in action, God on the prowl, God in motion toward us. We rarely walk away from conversations with the Trinity without a limp.

I therefore can't help being suspicious of much of the current talk about "keeping Sabbath" and attempts to reinvigorate the Sabbath as a Christian discipline. Jesus was crucified, in part, for being a notorious, well-documented Sabbath-breaker. Jesus never got into trouble because of the time he took off to be quiet. If Sabbath keeping is taking off time to listen to God, then it's a good thing. Otherwise, it's a tempting diversion. I fear the present enthusiasm for the Sabbath as a "spiritual practice" to be another attempt by modern people to slow down God's time, to somehow put a leash on the frenetic Trinity. As we have noted, much of modern thought had as its unstated goal to stabilize the world, to render time predictable, comprehensible, and safe so that we might better dominate a world now denuded of God.

Preaching dares to speak of another world, keeps a different time. Most sermons say what needs to be said and quit in only about twenty minutes. In faithful Christian preaching the preacher introduces a peculiar, particular, living God into the conversation of the congregation and then has the guts to get out of the way. As Barth said, "preachers dare." Our peculiar daring is to be willing instruments in God's incarnational undoing of time, to dare to have Easter redone.

The fun of being a preacher, over time—and sometimes the fear of being a preacher too—is to witness the lively intercourse between the exuberant Trinity and the poor old somnambulant church on a weekly basis. When the risen Christ gets up and walks among his people, you never know where he'll go. I delight in watching him shadow, seek, and stalk the poor, dumb, unwary laity. I never tire of the fireworks. Even now I feel a mingling of anticipation and anxiety rise in me as I think about next Sunday at eleven. I look forward to emptying myself into the Scriptures and getting lost in a biblical text, putting on the text as if it fit and strutting about a bit as a different person. Laying the text on them and then seeing who gets hit is great sport. And yet, to tell the truth, I'm also anxious concerning what God may try to pull off in some life by means of my next sermon. After four decades of sermons, I know enough about the Trinity to know that I never know what wild stunts God may attempt through preaching.

Only God knows what I'll be led to say in the sermon. Only God knows how the church will respond. Only God knows what God wants to do in us this Sunday. I only know for sure that God is out of my control. It is the nature of God to take over my sermons, to use me and refuse to be used by me. It is of the nature of the Trinity to say to the crucified Jesus, lying in the tomb, "Again!" The Trinity loves to reiterate itself. Preaching therefore demands kenosis of the preacher. It's out of my hands and yours too. God will have the last word.

In preaching, death's time keeps being undone, outdone, and Easter keeps being redone. *Maranatha!*

A Sermon: Last Easter

About that time King Herod laid violent hands upon some who belonged to the church. He had James, the brother of John, killed with the sword. After he saw that it pleased the Jews, he proceeded to arrest Peter also. (This was during the festival of Unleavened Bread.) When he had seized him, he put him in prison and handed him over to four squads of soldiers to guard him, intending to bring him out to the people after the Passover. While Peter was kept in prison, the church prayed fervently to God for him.

The very night before Herod was going to bring him out, Peter, bound with two chains, was sleeping between two soldiers, while guards in front of the door were keeping watch over the prison. Suddenly an angel of the Lord appeared and a light shone in the cell. He tapped Peter on the side and woke him, saying, "Get up quickly." And the chains fell off his wrists. The angel said to him, "Fasten your belt and put on your sandals." He did so. Then he said to him, "Wrap your cloak around you and follow me." Peter went out and followed him; he did not realize that what was happening with the angel's help was real; he thought he was seeing a vision. After they had passed the first and the second guard, they came before the iron gate leading into the city. It opened for them of its own accord, and they went outside and walked along a lane, when suddenly the angel left him. Then Peter came to himself and said, "Now I am sure that the Lord has sent his angel and rescued me from the hands of Herod and from all that the Jewish people were expecting."

As soon as he realized this, he went to the house of Mary, the mother of John whose other name was Mark, where many had gathered and were

> *praying. When he knocked at the outer gate, a maid named Rhoda came to answer. On recognizing Peter's voice, she was so overjoyed that, instead of opening the gate, she ran in and announced that Peter was standing at the gate. They said to her, "You are out of your mind!" But she insisted that it was so. They said, "It is his angel." Meanwhile Peter continued knocking; and when they opened the gate, they saw him and were amazed. He motioned to them with his hand to be silent, and described for them how the Lord had brought him out of the prison. And he added, "Tell this to James and to the believers." Then he left and went to another place.*
>
> *When morning came, there was no small commotion among the soldiers over what had become of Peter. When Herod had searched for him and could not find him, he examined the guards and ordered them to be put to death. Then [Peter] went down from Judea to Caesarea and stayed there.*
>
> *But the word of God continued to advance and gain adherents. (Acts 12:1-19, 24)*[30]

We had a great Easter, didn't we? Rented trumpets, a bank of lilies, TV. Crowd so large that we had to bring out extra chairs. Two of you graciously phoned to tell me how much you liked my sermon—and I'm sure many, many more of you intended to call. What an Easter!

But it didn't last. The next day I learned that American deaths in Iraq topped 4,400. Suicide bombings had doubled from the last year. While we were celebrating with Easter lilies and trumpeted "hallelujahs," Caesar reminded us who is really in charge. The real news was not from Jerusalem, but from Iraq, where a presumptively democratic Caesar dukes it out with a gaggle of allegedly terrorist Caesars. An Iraqi man whose son was shot dead by Blackwater mercenaries cried out for revenge; an entire wedding party was wiped out by a Taliban mine in Afghanistan. It's always the little, ordinary, powerless people on both sides who suffer for Caesar and who kill and who die for Caesar's Empire. Caesar has outdone us. Enough of Easter.

Easter never seems to last because the powers-that-be are determined to let death be the last word.

Easter once lasted fifty days; "the Great Fifty Days of Joy" the church called it. But that was then; this is now and Easter seems shorter every year. We have these great spiritual highs, predictably followed by these dismal, mediocre ecclesiastical lows. Bright Resurrection is overtaken by Grim Reality. Easter joy wilts even sooner than the florist's Easter lilies.

Jack Canfield is America's success guru, telling you how you can uplift yourself, by yourself. Yet even Canfield wrote a book entitled *After the Ecstasy the Laundry*. I don't care how high you jump, there is always the morning-after, the week-after, the fifty-days-after letdown.

But I'm not talking about that. I'm talking about the way Jesus' great Easter success gets wrestled from his people by Caesar so shortly after our victory celebration. It is as if a powerful policing makes sure that Easter is short-lived.

Up to this point in the Acts of the Apostles we've had quite a ride. The Holy Spirit wildly descended upon the church at Pentecost, shaking up everything, the Word of God leaping over all boundaries, overcoming all obstacles, spreading like wildfire over the whole world. All kinds of enemies, including Church Enemy Number One—Saul—have been brought to the faith. Is anything more powerful than the Word of God? Is there anything that's too much for the Holy Spirit?

Apparently, there is—the Empire. "About that time [that is, time just after Easter, that is, our time right now] Herod [lackey for the Caesar] laid violent hands upon . . . the church"—a polite Bible way of saying that Herod's soldiers went on murderous rampage. He killed James and, when he saw that his public opinion polls took an upward turn, he decided to kill Peter, the rock of the church, too. That's what kings do best—put powerless people to the sword. We didn't ask Iraq if they wanted to be liberated for democracy by us. When you have got the largest army in the world, you don't have to ask.

Herod has the largest army in the Near East (at least before Operation Iraqi Freedom) backing him up, so he doesn't ask, he tells. Peter, premier disciple, the first spokesman for the church, is in jail. Herod is going to shut up these talkative Galileans once and for all. Herod has imprisoned Peter during Passover, Israel's Fourth of July Independence Day celebration, just to show who's really in charge. But this is no minimum-security, executive prison. Peter is really, really in prison.

Peter is not only in chains; he is guarded by no less than four squads of soldiers. He's not only got guards outside his jail cell; he's forced to sleep between guards in the cell. He's really in jail. Peter is as good as dead.

And there's Peter pacing back and forth in his cell, terrified? No, this is Peter, the same one who fell asleep while Jesus was in anguish in Gethsemane. He's sleeping like a baby, dead to the world. As good as dead.

From out of nowhere an angel shows up, enters the cell, slaps Peter in the side, commands "Wake up! Get dressed!" Peter staggers about in a stupor. The angel leads him out of the cell as first one door, then another swings open before them. Peter, rubbing his eyes, now standing out in the street before the jail, says, "Hmm. I thought it was just a vision. This is for real!" (A curious comment, that one. You would think that Peter, as the "rock" of the church, would be a specialist in visions. But no, this is Peter, never noted for a surfeit of imagination.)

Peter scurries through darkened streets to Mary's house, where earnest prayer is being offered up to God for Peter by the church. Peter bangs on the door. (What kind of organization is this that meets in unmarried women's homes, and at night?)

While Peter bangs at the door, the little prayer group prays, "Lord, do something about Herod. And please consider helping poor Peter. Oh, Lord, please help, if it be thy will. And if it is not thy will, help us accept reality and adjust to our circumstances without complaint. Amen."

A maid, Rhoda, answers the knock, opens the door, sees Peter, and "in her joy" slams the door and runs to tell the prayer group, "Hey, he's loose! He's alive! He's here!"

And the church in unison responds, "You're nuts, Rhoda. You get back in the kitchen where you maids belong."

At last Peter stands undeniably before them, risen, free and then he disappears elsewhere. And the church in unison dumbfoundedly mutters, "Hmm, Rhoda was right."

Remind you of another story that we read here last Easter? Luke 22–24? Jesus wasn't just dead; he was crucified. Caesar at last shut him up by torturing him to death on a cross. And he wasn't just entombed. He was sealed shut with a big stone, with a squad of Caesar's finest to guard the tomb. (Soldiers making sure that a dead man doesn't go anywhere? Talk about waste in the military budget!)

And women were there too. Unarmed women came out in the darkness and, to their surprise and joy, discovered that God had defeated death and Caesar. The women ran back to the boys in Jerusalem shouting, "He's lose! He's free! God won!"

And the church with one voice responded, "You're nuts."

The first Easter preachers were joy-filled women. And the last people to believe in resurrection, when we get one, is the church—until Jesus himself knocked on our locked doors (John 20) and spoke to us, leading us to mutter, "So, the women were right?"

And we thought that was the last of Easter. But here in the Acts of the Apostles what we've got is Easter remade, *Deus redivivus*, resurrection repeated. You thought Easter was a once-and-for-all thing with Jesus. Well, think again. Easter lasts.

See? You thought Easter was over. You thought we heard the last of a powerful, victorious God last Easter. Well, think again. Easter keeps happening. All over town, jail cell doors are swinging open, the military is put in disarray, and haughty women like Rhoda are spreading seditious news.

Easter lasts. Easter isn't over until God says it's over.

Back when Peter preached to the street mob on Pentecost (Acts 2), Peter cited the prophet Joel. In the old days, God's Holy Spirit was out-poured upon just a few men named "prophets" who, with lively words, preached the mighty works of God, spoke truth to power, and made kings nervous. But there will come a day, said Joel, when God's Spirit will be poured out on old people, your sons and daughters, janitors and maids (that is, people who are usually silenced by the powerful). One day the once powerless will get to stand up and speak truth to power. That prom-ised day is fulfilled as maid Rhoda preaches Luke's second Easter sermon entitled, "Hey! He's Loose!"

The Resurrection is more even than the promise of eternal life for you and me after we die. Easter is the promise of the universal, cosmic tri-umph of God over all the forces of death and sin. Easter is whenever in the dark—out at the cemetery or at a prayer meeting at Mary's house— God dramatically demonstrates who's in charge. Easter is God's justice accomplished, God's kingdom come, God's will being done at last on earth as it is in heaven.

Luke ends this wild, wonderful Easter story by saying that there was quite a commotion at the Roman garrison in Jerusalem. "What in the world became of Peter?" they asked. And after an official court-martial, King Herod put the soldiers to death. As we said, that's what kings do. The only way Caesar knows to accomplish any good in the world is through violence. We are in Iraq only for good, noble reasons. It's crazy to die for a god but patriotic to die for a government. More people died in the twentieth century at the hands of their own governments than even those who died in war. All governments kill. That's how they do good. That's how they stay in charge.

But then, just when we thought that death had had the last word, God moves, kicks open the iron gate, slaps us in the side, gives us a vision, leads us into the darkness and through it, knocks on the door, turns the key in the lock, servant women begin to preach the good news, the church laughs at itself, and the word of God continues "to advance and gain adherents."[31] And despite our attenuated political imagination, it's Easter all over again.

Death-dealers, doom-doers, beware. You tried to shut Jesus up, once and for all. But you couldn't, and you can't. God is at last on the loose. The smart-mouthed talk continues. Prison doors swinging open; ordinary, powerless people speaking up like prophets; maids getting superior; death being defeated; and God getting back what belongs to God—and not just last Easter. Who's that knocking at our door? Easter continues. Easter lasts!

Epilogue: all you good church people, you now weeded-out, post-Easter elite, truly committed and naturally religious ones take note. The people most reluctant to believe in resurrection—when we get one—is us.

NOTES

Introduction

1. *Conversations with Barth on Preaching* (Nashville: Abingdon Press, 2006) and *Who Will Be Saved?* (Nashville: Abingdon Press, 2008). Thanks to my Abingdon editor, Dr. Robert Ratcliff, for his encouragement of the continuance of this conversation and for his wise editorial guidance. Thanks also to Drew Clayton, Stanley Hauerwas, Matt Fleming, Jenny Copeland, Tom Long, and Timothy Whitaker for their help with the manuscript.

1. New

1. Fred B. Craddock, *Overhearing the Gospel* (Nashville: Abingdon Press, 2002).

2. See the first half of S.K.'s *Philosophical Fragments*, trans. David Swenson (Princeton: Princeton University Press, 1962).

3. Looking back, the most important popular theological instigation of this ecclesiastical cult of the new was a decidedly anti-ecclesiastical book—Harvey Cox, *The Secular City: Secularization and Urbanization in Theological Perspective* (New York: Collier Books, 1965 [25th anniversary edition], 1990). Insouciance toward tradition, at least in the time of my own ministry, has its roots in this book's influence on my generation of mainline seminarians.

4. Having surveyed much of the past two centuries of homiletical thought, and a good deal of systematic theology of the same period, I find therein almost no interest in the chief concern of this book. "Again?" appears to be a problem solely for us contemporary preachers. That for the first time in the history of the church reiteration of the truth should be a problem for us is a commentary upon us.

5. Quoted by Robert Hughes, *The Shock of the New* (New York: Alfred A. Knopf, 1980), 9. I am indebted to Hughes for this material on the birth of the modern world (9–41).

6. That quintessential modern man, Mao Zedong, in one of his most famous poems, after noting that all the old Chinese emperors are dead, explains "only today are we men of feeling." We are the first generation to feel! Mao's feelings did not get in the way of his extermination of millions of Chinese. See *The Poems of Mao Zedong*, trans. Willis Barnstone (Berkeley: University of California Press, 2008), 78.

7. See Stephen Toulmin, *Cosmopolis: The Hidden Agenda of Modernity* (New York: Free Press, 1990).

8. Most of my ministry has been in a university setting. Throughout most of the history of the university, all professors, no matter which subject being taught, were historians. They felt obligated to pass on to the young what humanity had learned in order that the young, having learned what knowledge we have accumulated, could then advance knowledge. In recent years universities have become mostly adversaries with the past, generators of new trends. They are no longer the purveyors of the collective wisdom of others but rather the originators of fashion. C. John Sommerville says that today universities serve "the news," sell new ideas and information to their customers (students), much like newspapers. See C. John Sommerville, *The Decline of the Secular University* (New York: Oxford University Press, 2006).

9. Apollinaire's fellow writer Guy de Maupassant hated the Eiffel Tower, pronouncing it an ugly contraption of ladders and beams. He said that the tower ended in a ridiculous slender point that looked as if it ought to bear the statue of Atlas, though it basically ended in nothing. In a way, this huge finger pointing into nothingness was a fitting symbol for the modern era.

10. Richard Dawkins, *The God Delusion* (New York: Houghton Mifflin, 2006); Christopher Hitchens, *God Is Not Great: How Religion Poisons Everything* (New York: Hachette Book Group, 2007). A curious aspect of Dawkins and Hitchens is that they present their critique of theism as something fresh when their arguments are mostly rehash. If godlessness is such a sure sign of human advance, one would think that God would have been long dead at the hands of Nietzsche and Voltaire. Why enlist a writer for *Vanity Fair* to do what some of the greatest minds of the age failed to do?

11. David Tracy warns—or at least I suppose it to be a warning—that modern theologies "were principally determined not by the reality of God but by the *logos* of modernity" (*On Naming the Present: God, Hermeneutics and Church* [Maryknoll, N.Y.: Orbis Books, 1994], 41). There is no way a book about "keeping preaching fresh" would have been written by John Wesley. "Fresh" would surely be called "heresy."

12. Ted Smith, quoting Walter Benjamin, notes that the idea of progress is particularly fallacious when applied to "the historical process *as a whole.*" It may be accurate to speak of progress, but only in certain carefully limited situations. We can thus speak of progress in medicine or even in race relations in the United States but it would be ridiculous to say that America is "making progress" (Ted A. Smith, *The New Measures: A Theological History of Democratic Practice* [Cambridge: Cambridge University Press, 2007], 261–63). Christians don't believe in progress; we believe in redemption that comes in spite of our efforts.

13. For a definition of "Progressive Christianity" see http://www.tcpc.org. The website lists the "Eight Points of Progressive Christianity." There is also a magazine, *Progressive Christian*, which can be found online at tpcmagazine.org. As best I can discern, "progressive" in the context of this book is to be taken to mean the last gasp of nineteenth-century, social gospel liberalism.

14. Theology tends to be a bit like art in that there is no real "progress" in theological investigation. Art can be good, bad, tacky, trivial, or derivative but it can't really be "progressive."

15. Augustine, *Confessions* 11.14, trans. R. S. Pine-Coffin (London: Penguin Books, 1961), 264.

16. James W. McClendon, Jr., *Systematic Theology*, vol. 1 (Nashville: Abingdon Press, 1986), 17.

17. John Howard Yoder, *The Royal Priesthood: Essays Ecumenical and Ecclesiological* (Scottsdale, Pa.: Herald, 1998), 56, 55.

18. Aristotle, *Metaphysics* 1051b, 29–30.

19. William T. Cavanaugh, *Torture and Eucharist: Theology, Politics, and the Body of Christ* (Oxford: Blackwell, 1998), 222–23.

20. Charles Taylor, *A Secular Age* (Cambridge, Mass.: Harvard University Press, 2007).

21. Karl Barth, *Church Dogmatics*, III, 2, trans. T. H. L. Parker, et al. (Edinburgh, Scotland: T & T Clark, 1957), 522.

22. From "The Emptiness of Existence," in *Essays of Schopenhauer*, 2004 (retrieved March 6, 2009, from eBooks@Adelaide, ebooks.adelaide.edu.au).

23. Barth, *Church Dogmatics*, III, 2, 632.

24. As Barth says, the Gospel means, "we have time." *Church Dogmatics*, III, 2, 521.

25. The presentation of the Trinity as harmony, peace, and community (see part 2 of Catherine Mowry LaCugna, *God for Us* [San Francisco: HarperSanFrancisco, 1973]) may obscure the tendency of the Trinity to be disruptive of human appropriation of time.

26. In my church I have noted that most clergy, when they lead worship, tend to slow everything down—in their speech and movement—as if church action is always in slow motion. They tend to talk as if everyone in the congregation is either under five years old or over eighty. Is this unhurriedness a theological statement? Probably their slow pace is due to the majority of our clergy being senior citizens. Human life tends to slow down with age, even though our lives are moving more rap-

idly to their conclusion. Jesus did everything he needed to do, said everything he needed to say to save the world before he was thirty-five.

27. This is, I fear, what Reinhold Niebuhr called "Christian realism."

28. John Howard Yoder, *The Priestly Kingdom* (South Bend, Ind.: University of Notre Dame Press, 1984), 136–37.

29. Marcus Borg, *The Heart of Christianity: Rediscovering a Life of Faith* (San Francisco: Harper Collins, 2003), 178.

30. Our time seems normal, a "fact" to which we should adjust. In Proust's novels everything that time touches is killed by time; the wise get used to it. Death is normal. Yet as Michel Foucault taught us, in his observations of prisons, asylums, and hospitals, "normal" depends to a great extent on who has power in a society. In every society there is a "regime of truth" that determines what will be regarded as normal (*Power/Knowledge*, trans. Colin Gordon et al. [New York: Pantheon Books, 1980], 131). There is also a "regime of time" that declares the present as real. "Get real" is usually pronounced upon Christians by those who defend and benefit from the present order.

31. See the book by one of the heroes of the Progressive Christian movement, John Shelby Spong, *Why Christianity Must Change Or Die* (New York: HarperCollins Publishers, 1998). Spong's major problem with the God of Christiainity seems to be not only that God is old but also that the Christian claim that God actually does something in time.

32. "Progress" was disposed of as a Christian idea as far back as John Baillie's, *The Belief in Progress* (New York: Charles Scribner's Sons, 1951). Chesterton wrote that modern people say, "'Away with your old moral formulae; I am for progress.' Logically stated this means, 'Let us not settle what is good; but let us settle whether we are getting more of it'" (G. K. Chesterton, *Heretics* [New York: Devin Adair, 1950], 26).

33. Marva Dawn, *A Royal "Waste" of Time* (Grand Rapids: Eerdmans, 1999), 143. How different is Dawn's characterization of the prayer of the pastor than that of Sarah Coakley, in which she praises the "representational invisibility" of Anglican clergy who, now having no significance in English culture, have retreated to the quiet, restful, invisibility of personal prayer. "The Vicar at Prayer: an English Reflection on Ministry," *The Christian Century*, July 1, 2008. I fear that Coakley is attempting to give theological justification for clerical ineptitude.

34. P. T. Forsyth, *The Soul of Prayer* (Grand Rapids: Eerdmans, reprint of 1916), 91 (retrieved March 6, 2009, from http://www.oldlandmarks.com). Thanks to Bishop Tim Whitaker for pointing me to this.

35. "Nietzsche says that we will live the same life, over and over again. God—I'll have to sit through the Ice Capades again?" Woody Allen as quoted by Allan Hugh Cole Jr., *Be Not Anxious: Pastoral Care of Disquieted Souls* (Grand Rapids: Eerdmans, 2008), 28.

36. Kierkegaard noted that union with the God of Jews and Christians occurs not through our "elevation" but by God's "descent" (*Philosophical Fragments*, trans. David Swenson [Princeton: Princeton University Press, 1962], 39). See in this same volume S.K.'s parable of the king who showed his love for a maiden by disguising himself and descending to her, 32–35.

37. Robert Jenson, *Systematic Theology* (New York: Oxford University Press, 1977), Vol. 1, 217–18. Jenson says this in connection with an examination of the idea of time in Karl Barth's *Church Dogmatics*.

38. "[L]iberal modernity can best be seen as an energetic reaction to a particular and problematic version of nominalist Christianity. Early modernity saw itself as a salutary response to oppressive and obscurantist strains in Christian culture, but since it was reacting to a corruption of true Christianity [that is, Fundamentalism], it itself became similarly distorted and exaggerated" (Robert Barron, *The Priority of Christ: Toward a Postliberal Catholicism* [Grand Rapids: Brazos, 2007], 13). Michael Pasquarello III demonstrates the ways in which much so-called Evangelical Christianity is liberal modernity redone. See *Christian Preaching: A Trinitarian Theology of Proclamation* (Grand Rapids: Baker Academic, 2006).

39. Marcus J. Borg, *The Heart of Christianity: Rediscovering a Life of Faith* (New York: HarperCollins, 2003), 39.

40. Rick Warren, *The Purpose Driven Life: What on Earth Am I Here For?* (Grand Rapids: Zondervan, 2002), 6.

41. Neil Postman, *Technopoly: The Surrender of Culture to Technology* (New York: Vintage Books, 1993).

42. Dietrich Bonhoeffer, *Worldly Preaching,* ed. Clyde E. Fant (Nashville and New York: Thomas Nelson, 1975), 125.

43. Stanley Hauerwas helped me see how progressive/evangelical Christianity, in reducing the faith to "the message" made Christianity Gnostic: "In such a 'modernity' Christians have found it next to impossible to avoid the presumption that Christianity is a set of beliefs necessary to make their lives 'meaningful.' Conservative and liberal Christians believe that they have a personal relationship with God, a relation often associated with a decisive event or experience, which may or may not be enhanced by going to church. The crucial presumption is that 'going to church' is clearly not at the heart of what it means to be a Christian. Therefore modernity names the time in which Christians have found it almost impossible to avoid the spiritualization of their faith. Ironically, many Christians, who identify themselves as 'conservative,' that is, who assume it is very important that they have been 'saved,' fail to understand that their understanding of Christianity shares much with ancient Gnosticism" (Stanley Hauerwas, "The Gospel and Cultural Formations," *The State of the University: Academic Knowledges and the Knowledge of God* [Oxford: Blackwell, 2007], 39). Thomas G. Long has labeled Borg a "new Gnostic."

44. I believe that much of my critique of "PowerPoint preaching" also applies to preaching without notes. In attempting to preach without reference to any premeditated "script," the preacher tends severely to limit what is preached. The medium (the desire to appear to be speaking "from the heart," or extemporaneously) limits the message. I just heard a preacher give a long sermon without ever looking up from his manuscript. While he might have flunked "communication," it was obvious to everyone that what he was speaking about was hard, heavy, and demanded careful thought and consideration—a rarity in the "communication" from most contemporary pulpits. We preachers ought therefore to be reminded that sometimes we fail to gain a hearing not only because of the way we say something but also because we have so little to say.

45. Communications theorist James Carey says that a market-driven economy has accelerated our expectations for instant communication. "Communication" becomes the efficient delivery of goods across great distances to a receptive market. This modern view of communication, says Carey, "derives from one of the most ancient of human dreams: the desire to increase the speed and effect of messages as they travel in space" (*Communication as Culture: Essays on Media and Society* [New York: Routledge, 1992], 17).

46. Toward the end of his *Ethics* Barth notes the curious freedom that is to be found in art and in humor that releases us from "the seriousness of the present" (*Ethics* [New York: Seabury Press, 1981], 510). I can't imagine how anyone who knows much history could be too serious about the present. Christians find humor in the present, refusing to take the present too seriously on the basis of our convictions about the future.

47. John the Baptist said that with the coming of Jesus, there is judgment. The axe is laid to the root of the tree (Matt 3:10/ Luke 3:9). This parable contains the only other use of the verb to "cut out" (*ekkopto*).

2. Time's Thief

1. Billy Pilgrim, the protagonist in *Slaughterhouse-Five,* is introduced as one who is "unstuck in time," that is, a pilgrim.

2. "Fresh Air with Terry Gross: Writers Speak," 2004 WHYY Inc., Highbridge Company, disc 1.

3. Erich Auerbach said that Scripture, unlike Homer, does not want to "merely make us forget our own reality for a few hours. Scripture seeks to overcome our reality: we are to fit our own life into its world, feel ourselves to be elements in its structure of universal history" (*Mimesis: The Representation of Reality in Western Literature* [Princeton: Princeton University Press, 1968], 15). My point is that Scripture wants to overcome not only our reality but our time as well.

4. Kierkegaard, master of the ironic, mocked humanity's assumption (in the voice of the aesthete, Johannes Climacus) that the only way modern people would have taken notice of God is "if God had taken the form . . . of a rare, enormously large green bird, with a red beak, that perched on a tree . . . and perhaps even whistled in an unprecedented manner" (Søren Kierkegaard, *Concluding Unscientific Postscript to "Philosophical Fragments,"* Vol. I, [Princeton: Princeton University Press, 1992], 245).

5. Kierkegaard, once again, presciently saw the sinful evasion within our "history." He asks, in the frontispiece of *Philosophical Fragments*, how "is it possible to base an eternal happiness upon historical knowledge?" later ridiculing the "Disciple at Second Hand" (ch. 5). As I write this I learn that Thomas Nelson Company has produced a "Chronological Study Bible" in which Scripture has been cut and pasted into a coherent historical narrative. I assume that if biblical redactors had wanted to produce a coherent historical narrative, they could have. Instead, they produced distinctively nonchronological narratives like the Gospel of Mark.

6. I fear that's one thing that Kierkegaard missed in his exploration of boredom as the great modern curse. S.K. usually recommends some form of self-renovation, self-awareness, or self-modification as the means of overcoming boredom. I believe that boredom is the inevitable result of a world bereft of God and that its only cure is a living, surprising God.

7. Walter Benjamin says that the modern world invented "homogeneous, empty time" in which time, no longer something determined by God's providence, was conceived of as a matter of unvarying linear progression. See Walter Benjamin, *Illuminations* (New York: Schocken Books, 1968), 263–64. I wonder if medieval people got bored? Perhaps boredom is a peculiarly modern malady, a byproduct of a world in which there is no God to make even our times of inactivity interesting?

8. Proust, *Remembrance of Things Past*, III 737n, VI 68.

9. Cited in note number 1, frontispiece.

10. Karl Barth, *Church Dogmatics*, IV, 3, trans. T. H. L. Parker, et al. (Edinburgh, Scotland: T & T Clark, 1957), 327.

11. Barth, *Church Dogmatics*, I, 1, 464.

12. This is Robert Jenson's wonderful way of putting the matter. Robert W. Jenson, *Systematic Theology*, Vol. 1, *The Triune God* (New York: Oxford University Press, 1997), 42–44.

13. Pope Benedict opened his second encyclical with the claim that "a distinguishing mark of Christians is the fact that they have a future" (*First Things* [February 2008]: 55).

14. Barth speaks of Jesus' resurrection as an "eternal" event that is contemporary with each believer, so much so that we can no longer ascribe the resurrection to a temporal timeframe. Past, present, and future have little meaning when speaking of an event like the resurrection, which obliterates such humanly constructed distinctions (Karl Barth, *Church Dogmatics*, I, 291, 308).

15. Karl Barth, *Theology in Church* (New York: Harper and Bros., 1962), 61.

16. Ibid.

17. Kierkegaard, *Philosophical Fragments*, Ch. V.

18. See chapter 1 of Franz Overbeck, *On the Christianity of Theology*, trans. John E. Wilson (San Jose, Calif.: Pickwick Publications, 2002).

19. Karl Barth, "The Strange New World within the Bible" (1916), *Word of God and the Word of Man*, 28–50.

20. Early in *Romans*, Barth dismisses "history" as "the display of the supposed advantages of power and intelligence which some men possess over others." Then he says, "The judgment of God is the end of history" (77). English translation by Edwyn C. Hoskyns, Karl Barth, *The Epistle to the Romans* (London: Oxford University Press, 1933), 77.

21. Barth, *Church Dogmatics*, IV, 3, 338.

22. Barth, *Church Dogmatics*, III, 2, 552.

23. Ibid., 456.

24. Barth, *Church Dogmatics*, II, 2, 516.

25. Barth, *Church Dogmatics*, IV, 1, 505. Ernst Troeltsch had argued that history should be "democratized," that Jewish and Christian history must be made analogous to all other history in order to be studied as history in the modern German university. Thus Jewish and Christian history could not be studied by modern historians until God was rendered mute and inoperative as an agent in history. See the essay by Scott Bader-Saye in Rand Rashkover and C. C. Pecknold, eds., *Liturgy, Time, and the Politics of Redemption* (Grand Rapids: Eerdmans, 2006), 94–95. Barth, writing in the aftermath of Troeltsch, argued the opposite: you can't understand anything about what's going on in history until Scripture teaches you that salvation history is "related to world history as a whole. It is the center and the key to all events" (Barth, *Church Dogmatics*, III, 3, 186).

26. Barth, *Church Dogmatics*, IV, 2, 471.

27. Ibid., 473.

28. Barth, *Church Dogmatics*, III, 4, 587.

29. Barth, *Church Dogmatics*, II, 1, 616.

30. Barth, *Church Dogmatics*, I, 2, 45–55. Also, Barth writes beautifully, in *Romans*, of Jesus Christ as the point where eternity and time intersect: "In this name two worlds meet and go apart, two planes intersect, the one known and the other unknown. The known plane is God's creation, fallen out of its union with Him, . . . the world of men, and of time, and of things—our world. This known plane is intersected by another plane that is unknown—the world of the Father, of the Primal Creation, and of the final Redemption. The relation between us and God, between this world and [God's] world, presses for recognition, but the line of intersection is not self-evident. The point on the line of intersection at which the relation becomes observable and observed is Jesus, Jesus of Nazareth, the historical Jesus" (Karl Barth, *The Epistle to the Romans*, trans. E. C. Hoskyns [London: Oxford University Press, 1933], 29).

31. Barth, *Church Dogmatics*, IV, 2, 544.

32. Karl Barth, *The Christian Life* (Grand Rapids: Eerdmans, 1981), 236.

33. Barth, *Romans*, 145–46.

34. Barth, *Church Dogmatics*, I, 2, 55.

35. Barth, *Church Dogmatics*, IV, 3, 362–63.

36. Barth, *Church Dogmatics*, III, 2, 477. The resurrection is such a rebuke to the notion of "history" or "fact of history" that historical details of the resurrection "are irrelevant" says Barth in *Romans* (204). Preoccupation with historical questions, related to the resurrection, are for Barth "seeking the living among the dead" (205).

37. Barth, *Church Dogmatics*, III, 2, 465.

38. In college I was made to read Martin Heidegger, *Being and Time* (translated by Joan Stambaugh [Albany: State University of New York Press, 1953]). I remember even then being stunned by the recognition that my being—my actually existing in time—was something that was not given. It was something that must be achieved, wrought by me in time. This was too great an assignment for a college sophomore. Yet it did raise the question of time and its significance, a question that I'm pursuing forty years later. My pursuit is a reminder that the human psyche is rarely over and done with ideas once one has them. To have an idea as a sophomore in college sometimes requires patience in waiting to really "have" the idea until one is sixty! I think this is relevant to the discussion of this book. Some ideas are good enough to take at least forty years before they are ours.

39. Rudolf Bultmann, *Theology of the New Testament*, trans. K. Grobel (New York: Charles Scribner's Sons, 1951), 22.

40. As Bultmann noted, modern people believe that they are "self-subsistent" and "immune from the interference of supernatural powers." This is not only a challenge to the notion of eschatology, which is a dramatic instance of "interference of supernatural powers" but also a challenge for preaching. The challenge of Christian preaching in modernity, taught Bultmann, is to submit preaching to

the standards of modernity in the hope that something can be retrieved that can be received by modern people. See Rudolf Bultmann, *Kerygma and Myth: A Theological Debate* (New York: Harper and Bros., 1961), 7.

41. Bultmann, *Kerygma and Myth: A Theological Debate*, 130.

42. By switching from the Jewish, incarnate, historical rooting of the gospel to the existentialist, rather Gnostic distortion of the gospel, Bultmann had granted Gotthold Lessing's "ugly, broad ditch" between faith and history that "Accidental truths of history can never become the proof of necessary truths of reason." See Gotthold Lessing, "On the Proof of the Spirit and Power," *Lessing's Theological Writings*, trans. Henry Chadwick (Stanford, Calif.: Stanford University Press, 1957).

43. In his book, *A Theology of History* (San Francisco: Ignatius Press, 1994), Hans Urs von Balthasar notes that for an act to have any real ethical significance, it must occur in real time. When one attempts to look at history in a timeless fashion—such as occurs in Marx—real human agency is undercut. Therefore, when Bultmann presents the Christian faith as needing demythologizing, he is talking about lifting the Christian faith out of time, defeating Christianity's time-bound quality. But the result is to destroy utterly the human agent, because the human agent can only have significance in history, in time. Plato is a difficult mistake to overcome, in this regard.

44. Walter Brueggemann, *The Prophetic Imagination* (Philadelphia: Fortress Press, 1993), 60.

45. Karl Barth loved this text, "wait for and hasten." He preached numerous sermons on this text and referred to it frequently in *Romans*. In a 1917 sermon (April 29) he calls this phrase, "hurry up and wait for" "unapproachable, a jubilation as if sung by angel choirs, . . . a great rumble as if from a far off thunderstorm."

46. Tom Long, "Imagine There's No Heaven: The Loss of Eschatology in American Preaching," *Journal of Preachers* (Advent 2006): 26–27.

47. This point is worked so well by Reinhard Hutter in his contrast of "utopian" and "pneumatic" eschatology in "Ecclesial Ethics, the Church's Vocation, and Practice," *Pro Ecclesia* 2, no. 4 (Fall): 435. Karl Barth repeatedly rejected "natural theology" as inadequate for the radical disruption of nature in the Atonement. I am arguing here that a sense of time as "natural"—tied to the cyclic passage of the seasons, is inadequate to account for what has happened to our time in Jesus Christ.

48. I wonder if part of the appeal of "narrative homiletics," in which the connection between preaching and narrative was stressed (Aristotle defined a story as having a beginning, middle, and end) was yet another attempt on the part of us preachers to stabilize God's eschatological time into a more tamed and orderly experience of time. Eugene Lowry's *Homiletical Plot* (Atlanta: John Knox Press, 1980) notes how good sermons move through time. But Lowry's is ordered, sequential time. Note that Scripture often begins its narratives without context, introduction, and often ends without tidy conclusions. Encouraged by Scripture, I believe that sermons ought to have a beginning, middle, and end, but not necessarily in that order. James W. Thompson charges that not only does narrative homiletics (such as Lowry fostered) erroneously assume a Christian culture but also aims at the listeners' affirmation rather than transformation, has little ethical content, and fails to form Christian community. See James W. Thompson, *Preaching Like Paul: Homiletical Wisdom for Today* (Louisville: Westminster John Knox Press, 2001), 9–14.

49. So Robert Jenson says that the main difference between a living God and a dead one is that a living God can still surprise you. In these last paragraphs, I'm heavily indebted to Robert W. Jenson, *Systematic Theology: The Triune God*, Vol. 1 (Oxford: Oxford University Press, 1997), especially 194–227.

50. Karl Barth, *Prayer According to the Catechisms of the Reformation*, trans. S. F. Terrien (Philadelphia: Westminster Press, 1952), 236.

51. I suspect that one reason we attempt to "spiritualize" Easter, making it into a religious phenomenon rather than to receive Easter as the political fact that the gospels claim it to be, is as an attempt not to change our intellectual paradigms. We attempt to think about the resurrection using modern ways of thinking. Yet modern ways of thinking were born, in great part, out of an attempt to exclude the resurrection from the realm of truth. Modern paradigms of knowledge tend to be

subservient to the present political order. So we can't think about Easter without conversion of our politics and our ways of thinking. We Easter preachers really have our work cut out for us.

3. Repetition

1. In some ways, this text is the whole argument of this book. By the way, is it significant that Jesus says the faithful scribe first brings out what is "new" before bringing out what is "old?" Our usual order is "old," then "new." Jesus, on the other hand, recommends getting the new out of the way first so we can move to the substantive old.

2. Father James Lindler overheard one of his young congregants reporting his most recent sermon: "It was just like all of Father Lindler's sermons, 'Blah, blah, blah, love.'" Lindler took this as a compliment. (Sermon recorded on *Day One Podcast*, May 17, 2008.)

The cumulative effect of preaching is but one of the reasons it is important for pastors to be stationed in a church long enough for their preaching to burrow into the souls of their listeners. Gospel preaching takes time. John Leith says that Protestantism began not only by asking, "How can I find a gracious God?" the typically Lutheran account of the Reformation, but also by asking the more Reformed question "Where can I find the true church?" If the church is constituted by preaching, we must have preachers who are willing to locate, commit, and preach to a congregation enough Sundays until a faithful church has time to be gathered around the Word. See John Leith, *From Generation to Generation* (Louisville: Westminster John Knox Press, 1990), 55.

3. Walter Brueggemann, *Reverberations of Faith: A Theological Handbook of Old Testament Themes* (Louisville: Westminster John Knox Press, 2002), 222.

4. Richard B. Hays, *Echoes of Scripture in the Letters of Paul* (New Haven, Conn.: Yale University Press, 1989), 167, emphasis is original.

5. Walt Whitman, *Leaves of Grass* (Boston: Small, Maynard, & Company, 1905), 78; see also T. S. Eliot's thoughts on repetition in "Four Quartets: East Coker," III, *Collected Poems 1909–1962* (New York: Harcourt Brace Jovanovich, 1962).

6. Two management consultants have told me that one of the weaknesses in my leadership style is that I don't "stay on target." I have difficulty "staying focused," "sticking with the message." My fourth-grade teacher could have told me as much. My mind wanders. My tastes are catholic in nature. I'm interested in too many different things. The consultants were telling me that, in service to the organization I'm attempting to lead I must submit to the needs of the organization. In short, I must be willing again and again, to repeat myself.

7. Roughly equivalent to Louis Armstrong's statement about jazz: "If you have to ask, I can't explain it to you."

8. Kierkegaard noted that for Plato "Truth is not introduced into the individual from without, but was within him." Truth behaves exactly the opposite in Christianity, coming within from without. As John says of Jesus, "He came unto his own and his own knew him not." See Søren Kierkegaard, *Philosophical Fragments*, trans. David F. Swenson (Princeton: Princeton University Press, 1962), 11.

9. Stanley M. Hauerwas has long stressed that one of the characteristics of distinctively Christian speech is that it is "habituated"—formed in us through habits over time and that one of the chief roles of the pastor is to teach us good habits in our use of speech: "To learn to speak Christian, to learn to speak well as a Christian, is to be habituated. Thus we are told we must speak the truth in love. The love that we believe necessary to make our words true is not a subjective attitude, but rather, is to be formed by the habits of the community necessary for the Church to be a true witness" ("Carving Stone or Learning to Speak Christian," *The State of the University: Academic Knowledges and the Knowledge of God* [Oxford: Blackwell Publishing, 2007], 120).

10. Norman Mailer, with Michael Lennon, *On God: An Uncommon Conversation* (New York: Random House, 2007), 122–23.

11. Bruce F. Kawin, *Telling It Again and Again: Repetition in Literature and Film* (Ithaca, N.Y.: Cornell University Press, 1972), 4.

12. For a wonderfully illustrated discussion of repetition and aesthetics, see especially Maria H. Loh's *Titian Remade: Repetition and the Transformation of Early Modern Italian Art* (Los Angeles: Getty Publication, 2007).

13. Most of my information on rhetoric comes from Edward P. J. Corbett, *Classical Rhetoric for the Modern Student* (New York: Oxford University Press, 1990), "Figures of Speech," 424–62.

14. The following list of terms from the classical study of rhetoric come from Dr. Gideon Burton, of Brigham Young University: http://rhetoric.byu.edu/.

15. Richard Lischer's *The Preacher King: Martin Luther King and the Word That Moved America* (Oxford: Oxford University Press, 1997) has a wonderful rhetorical analysis of King's preaching that stresses his use of the various figures of speech of repetition. See chapter 5.

16. Søren Kierkegaard, *Fear and Trembling: Repetition*, trans. Howard V. Hong (Princeton: Princeton University Press, 1983).

17. Søren Kierkegaard, *Either/Or*, Vol. 1, trans. David F. Swenson and Lillian Marvin Swenson (Garden City, N.Y.: Anchor Books, 1959), 70.

18. I think he was pointing to the truth of Heraclitus's we-can't-step-in-same-river-twice.

19. Kierkegaard, *Repetition*, 131. I am told that in Danish, the word *repetition* (*gjentagelse*) means not simply "to repeat" but also "to take back."

20. Søren Kierkegaard, *Christian Discourses*, trans. Walter Lowrie (New York: Oxford University Press, 1961), 371–77.

21. I take issue with S.K. in his urging us to will ourselves into the Christian story—God in the power of the Holy Spirit wills us to be part of the Christian story—we don't have to want very much to understand the gospel in order to be given the gift of the gospel. I am routinely impressed by those people in my congregation who aren't particularly earnest about hearing God speak to them who have God speak to them.

22. Karl Barth, *Church Dogmatics*, II, 1, trans. T. H. L. Parker, et al. (Edinburgh, Scotland: T & T Clark, 1957), 250. The young Barth was greatly influenced by Kierkegaard. I cannot determine that Barth was influenced by S.K.'s *Repetition*, though the similarities between this theme in Barth and in S.K. are striking.

23. Stanley M. Hauerwas, *With the Grain of the Universe* (Grand Rapids: Brazos Press, 2001), 173–74.

24. In *Church Dogmatics*, IV, 1, 3, Barth introduces the metaphor of a circle to depict the complex structure of *Church Dogmatics* as unified whole.

25. Barth, *Church Dogmatics*, IV, 1, 281.

26. Ibid.

27. Ibid.

28. Ibid., 76.

29. Ibid., 295–96.

30. Karl Barth, *The Doctrine of the Word of God*, *Church Dogmatics*, I, 1, trans. G. T. Thompson (Edinburgh, Scotland: T & T Clark, 1936), 57.

31. Thomas G. Long, *The Witness of Preaching* (Louisville: Westminster John Knox Press, 1989), 25.

32. Flannery O'Connor, "The Nature and Aim of Fiction," *Mystery and Manners: Occasional Prose*, eds. Sally and Robert Fitzgerald (New York: Farrar, Straus, and Giroux, 1961).

33. Barth, *Church Dogmatics*, II, 1, 250.

34. Is the recent interest (following Aristotle's concern for *ethos*) in the character of preacher an aspect of a homiletics that has become less interested in the Agent of preaching (God in Jesus Christ, in the power of the Holy Spirit)? The most interesting (and troublingly difficult) character in preaching is the Trinity. The character of preachers is mainly of interest in how the curious character of God impacts the preacher's character. We preachers are never as interesting as the God whom we preach.

35. N. T. Wright, *New Testament and the People of God* (London: SPCK, 1992), 140.

36. Wittgenstein said, "You can't hear God speak to someone else, you can hear him only if you are being addressed." Scripture is not really God's word, lying on the printed page. It is God's word as address, summons, vocation, a dynamic that is most likely to happen in preaching. When generalized, abstract "God's Word" becomes God's address to you, that's truly "God's Word" (Wittgenstein as quoted by David B. Burrell, *Deconstructing Theodicy: Why Job Has Nothing to Say to the Puzzle of Suffering* [Grand Rapids: Brazos Press, 2008], 49).

37. Barth, *Church Dogmatics*, IV, 1, 648.

38. Ibid., 608.

39. Karl Barth, *Homiletics* (Louisville: Westminster John Knox, 1991), 44.

40. "Four Quartets," T. S. Eliot, *Collected Poems 1909–1962* (New York: Harcourt Brace Jovanovich, 1962), 188–89.

41. Scripture makes Jesus' encounter with hometown sickness and death an even greater challenge: the little girl is dead. Levitical law says that the dead are not to be touched, for the dead defile (Lev 21). As for the good-as-dead anonymous woman with the discharge of blood, Scripture suggests that she is in this fix because she must have failed to be righteous. She wouldn't be sick if she had not done something wrong, so she is probably an outcast from the faith community, that is, *us* (Lev 15:25-30).

4. Time Disrupted

1. *God's Companions: Reimagining Christian Ethics* (Oxford: Blackwell, 2006), 34.

2. John Calvin, "The Sense of Deity Found in All Men," *On the Christian Faith: Selections from the Institutes, Commentaries, and Tracts*, ed. John T. McNeill (New York: Bobbs-Merrill, 1957), 9.

3. See chapter 1 in Arthur Waley, *The Way and Its Power: A Study of the Tao Te Ching and Its Place in Chinese Thought* (London: Allen & Unwin, 1934; New York: Grove, 1958).

4. Bonhoeffer speaks of the way Scripture reads us into the gospel: "They [the biblical books] set the listening fellowship in the midst of the wonderful world of revelation of the people of Israel with its prophets, judges, kings, and priests, its wars, festivals, sacrifices, and sufferings. The fellowship of believers is woven into the Christmas story, the baptism, the miracles and teaching, the suffering, dying, and rising again of Jesus Christ. It participates in the very events that occurred on this earth for the salvation of the world, and in doing so receives salvation in Jesus Christ. . . . It is not that God is the spectator and sharer of our present life, howsoever important that is; but rather that we are the reverent listeners and participants in God's action in the sacred story, the history of the Christ on earth." Preachers attempt to do what Scripture does. See Bonhoeffer, *Life Together* (New York: Harper and Bros., 1954), 53–54.

5. Calvin, "The Sense of Deity Found in All Men," 17.

6. Wallace A. Bacon, *The Art of Interpretation* (New York: Holt, Reinhart & Winston, 1979), 38, as quoted in Jana Childers and Clayton J. Schmit, *Performance in Preaching: Bringing the Sermon to Life* (Grand Rapids: Baker Academic, 2008), 31.

7. John Calvin, *On the Christian Faith*, ed. John T. McNeill (New York: Bobbs-Merrill, 1957), 23.

8. So Barth said that preachers "realize how impossible their action is, but they may still look beyond its uncertainty and focus on the fact of revelation. This will give them confidence that the revealed will of God which is at work in their action will cover their weakness and corruptness. . . . Knowing the forgiveness of sins, they may do their work in simple obedience, no longer then, as a venture, but in the belief that God has commanded it" (*Homiletics*, trans. Geoffrey W. Bromiley and Donald E. Daniels [Louisville: Westminster John Knox Press, 1991], 69–70).

9. Marilynne Robinson, *The Death of Adam: Essays on Modern Thought* (New York: Picador, 98), 230–31.

10. Barbara K. Lundblad, *Marking Time: Preaching Biblical Stories in the Present Tense* (Nashville: Abingdon Press, 2007).

11. Sixth note from the "Notes on the Translation of Greek Tenses," just after the preface to *The New American Standard Bible, New Testament* (Cleveland and New York: World Publishing Company, 1960).

12. John Calvin, *On the Christian Faith: Selections from the Institutes, Commentaries, and Tracts*, trans. John T. McNeill (New York: Bobbs-Merrill, 1967), 17.

13 Here I'm being instructed by Gerhard Ebeling, *God and Word*, trans. James W. Leitch (Philadelphia: Fortress Press, 1967), particularly 17–19.

14. As Charles L. Campbell says, "Not only is the preacher's *message* shaped by the story of Jesus . . . but the very *act* of preaching itself is a performance of Scripture, an embodiment of God's reign after the pattern of Jesus. . . . Preachers accept a strange kind of powerlessness, which finally relies on God to make effective not only individual sermons, but the very practice of preaching . . . the preacher's words must be 'redeemed by God' " (*Preaching Jesus: New Directions for Homiletics in Hans Frei's Postliberal Hermeneutic* [Grand Rapids: Eerdmans, 1997], 214, emphasis in original).

15. Neil Postman, *Amusing Ourselves to Death* (New York: Penguin, 1985).

16. "The Vacation," Wendell Berry, *The Selected Poems of Wendell Berry* (Berkeley, Calif.: Counterpoint, 1998), 157.

17. "As the church speaks and hears the gospel and as the church responds in prayer and confession, the church's life is a great conversation, and this conversation is none other than our anticipatory participation in the converse of the Father and the Son in the Spirit; as the church is enlivened and empowered by this hearing and answer, the inspiration is none other than the Spirit who is the life between the Father and the Son" (Robert W. Jenson, *Systematic Theology: The Triune God*, Vol. I [Oxford: Oxford University Press, 1997], 228).

18. Quoted by John W. Wright, *Telling God's Story: Narrative Preaching for Christian Formation* (Downers Grove, Ill.: IVP Academic, 2007), 23. I am indebted to Wright for much of the discussion on hermeneutics that follows.

19. Quoted by Wright, *Telling God's Story*, 29.

20. What I am claiming for homiletical repetition of texts is close to what Walter Brueggemann has said: "The text lingers. Out of that lingering, however, from time to time, words of the text characteristically erupt into new usage. . . . What has been tradition, hovering in dormancy, becomes available experience" (Walter Brueggemann, *Texts That Linger, Words That Explode: Listening to Prophetic Voices* [Minneapolis: Fortress Press, 2000], 1).

21. Written with Rowan Greer, *Early Biblical Interpretation* (Philadelphia: Westminster Press, 1986).

22. My stress on divine agency is, of course, indebted to Karl Barth whose *The Word of God and the Word of Man*, trans. Douglas Horton (New York: Harper and Bros., 1928) recovered for modern theology a sense of the Word of God as active and fecund.

23. As quoted by Gardner Taylor in Don M. Wardlaw, *Preaching Biblically: Creating Sermons in the Shape of Scripture* (Philadelphia: Westminster Press, 1983), 137.

24. Dietrich Bonhoeffer, *Life Together* (New York: Harper and Bros., 1954), 44.

25. In Romans 10:14-21.

26. Barth's conviction of the primacy of preaching is discussed well by Stephen Webb, *The Divine Voice: Christian Proclamation and the Theology of Sound* (Grand Rapids: Brazos, 2004), 176–78. James Simpson, *Burning to Read: English Fundamentalism and Its Reformation Opponents* (Cambridge, Mass.: Harvard University Press, 2007) shows that evangelical Christians made a mistake in privileging the written over the oral word, in allowing print to dominate their encounters with Scripture. Print, by its nature, excludes, circumscribes, and limits what is communicated to itself. The embrace of the "literal sense" of Scripture led to modern Fundamentalism and its problems, a sort of a-theistic reading of Scripture. As Simpson says, "only oral or unwritten context made sense of written texts." In other words, Scripture—printed and static—must have preaching to make it make *theological* sense.

27. Walter Brueggemann, *Texts That Linger, Words That Explode: Listening to Prophetic Voices*, ed. Patrick D. Miller (Minneapolis: Fortress Press, 2000), 41.

28. David Buttrick, "The Language of Jesus," *Theology Today*, Vol. 64 (2008): 423–44.

29. Paul Berliner says that boredom is a major impetus for artistic creativity. A jazz composer like Thelonious Monk constantly improvises because of "the monotony of repeated performance routines." Singer Carmen Lundy says, "After you have sung a song one hundred and fifty times, the chances are that you are going to begin doing little, different things with it" (Paul F. Berliner, *Thinking in Jazz: The Infinite Art of Improvisation* [Chicago: University of Chicago Press, Chicago Studies in Ethnomusicology, 1994], 96). Thanks to Drew Clayton for pointing me to Berliner's book.

30. Why was this fecund story omitted from the *Revised Common Lectionary?* I can only surmise that the reason for exclusion was political—the Lectionary Committee was mostly Republican.

31. I love the way the old Revised Standard Version rendered this Greek phrase as "The Word grew and multiplied"—like rabbits, God's Word proliferated.

INDEX OF NAMES

INDEX OF SCRIPTURE